UNCONDITIONAL
LOVE

UNCONDITIONAL
LOVE

RADICAL STORIES. REAL PEOPLE.

B&H
PUBLISHING GROUP
NASHVILLE, TENNESSEE

978-1-4336-7971-1

Published by B&H Publishing Group
Nashville, Tennessee

Developmental Editor—Ben Stroup—Greenbrier, TN—
BenStroup.com

Dewey Decimal Classification: 361.2
Subject Heading: LOVE \ GENEROSITY \
CHRISTIAN LIFE

1 2 3 4 5 6 7 8 9 • 17 16 15 14 13

DEDICATION

To those with a desire to change the world:
May you find the courage to share love—
unconditionally—with those to who have
been given and who have been given to.

⌒

CONTENTS

This is My command:
Love one another as I have loved you.
No one has greater love than this,
That someone would lay down his life for his friends.

—Jesus (John 15:12–13)

The King will say to those on His right,
"Come, you who are blessed by My Father,
Inherit the kingdom prepared for you
From the foundation of the world.
For I was hungry and you gave Me something to eat;
I was thirsty and you gave Me something to drink;
I was a stranger and you took Me in;
I was naked and you clothed Me;
I was sick and you took care of Me;
I was in prison and you visited Me."

And the King will answer them, "I assure you:
Whatever you did for one of the
Least of these brothers of Mine,
You did for Me."

—Jesus (Matt. 25:34–36, 40)

Prayer of St. Francis of Assisi

Lord, make me an instrument of your peace.
Where there is hatred, let me sow love.
Where there is injury, pardon.
Where there is doubt, faith.
Where there is despair, hope.
Where there is darkness, light.
And where there is sadness, joy.

O Divine Master,
Grant that I may not so much seek to be consoled, as to console;
To be understood, as to understand;
To be loved, as to love.
For it is in giving that we receive.
It is in pardoning that we are pardoned.
And it is in dying that we are born to eternal life.
Amen.

Introduction

Unconditional Love Is Uncommon,
Not Impossible

L ove seems to hang in the balance of fairy tales and tragedies. It is one of the most misunderstood and misapplied words in our vocabulary. Love is so fluid that it can apply to your favorite ice cream flavor or in the next sentence refer to the feelings we have for another human being. It's easy to understand how so many find themselves confused when it comes to the subject of love.

This word rarely is received in its purest form. Instead, it comes with a tremendous amount of conditions, baggage, and confusion. Psychology tells us that the act of receiving, or not receiving, love can make or break a person emotionally and spiritually. It can propel us toward greatness or limit us in our capacity to find fulfillment, satisfaction, and purpose.

A church may be the only place you have ever heard the two words *unconditional* and *love* used together in the same sentence. We hear it most often talked about when we remember and reflect on the voluntary sacrifice of God's Son on the cross to pay the penalty of our sin. In turn, everyone has the ability to reconnect and have an ongoing, dynamic relationship with God. This is the ultimate expression of love without condition.

The idea that love might be unconditional is perplexing. Is that even possible? And who actually has the capacity to act in that way toward another human being? Most people have never experienced unconditional love. Too often, the affection of others comes at too high a price to even consider the possibility that love might be unconditional.

This notion of unconditional love dissipates in our attempt to act in this way toward others. We try with the best of intentions but end up projecting our expectations on others, only showing them favor and love when they satisfy our needs and follow through with our requests. We don't mean to act like this or behave in this way. It is just so part of our nature that we can't help ourselves.

Most of our life experiences, if we are honest with ourselves and others, teach us that we must do something to earn the love of others. We must do what our parents tell us to do. We must meet society's expectations for our level of education, personal achievement, financial success, etc. We must be the ideal spouse. We must be the prettiest, drive the fastest cars, work from corner offices in high-rise buildings, and be someone no one can live without. If we can achieve the right things and avoid the fatal pitfalls, then we have a shot at truly experiencing love, right?

The problem with this approach to love is that it sets us up for defeat. Sooner or later, because of something we have or have not done, we lose the love of someone or something and our world unravels. We disappoint our parents, our spouse, or our children. We experience financial difficulty or fail to get the promotion. Who is left to show us love? Sometimes, it is no one.

Worse, what if we are born into the wrong neighborhood? What if we never get access to quality health care and have to live with a disability or maligned body that might easily have been prevented, cured, or fixed? And what if our education is minimal at best? If we apply society's standards, who will love these people, not to mention what can they possibly do to receive the type of love that comes without condition?

The good news is that unconditional love is available to everyone. If God lives within us, then we have the capacity to show unconditional love toward others, even to the least of these. We know the pain of letting other people down, and we are aware of the pressure of constantly trying to earn the affection of others by doing things they will admire, acknowledge, and affirm. What if we decided to live life differently?

The way to receive unconditional love is to give it away. Unconditional love doesn't come with any expectations or strings attached. It is present whether or not we succeed or fail and isn't attached to what we do but to who we are.

That kind of love is unconditional. When we see it, experience it, or give it away, people take notice. And we have the capacity to show this love toward others because God has loved us in the same way.

Unconditional love is uncommon. Uncommon doesn't mean impossible; it just means uncommon. But God's plan has been uncommon from the beginning, so this isn't exactly new. When we break ranks with our culture and embrace an uncommon approach to love, we invite the opportunities into our everyday lives where we can extend unconditional love to others.

You don't have to start an international relief organization or have billions of dollars to give away to change the world. The reality is you can do that right where you are. You don't change cultures by influencing groups of people in masses. You change the world one person at a time.

It could be as simple as a handshake and a smile or as complex as raising funds to accomplish something specific. Whatever it is, we must recognize that we have the capacity to show unconditional love to others. And in doing so, we are transformed into agents of change.

Jesus could have fought an earthly battle and waged war on Rome. There were plenty of people, even some of His disciples, who would have preferred He take that approach. But when Jesus talked about the kingdom of God, He was clear that God's way of living is different from our way of living.

Our clearest picture of this uncommon, unconditional love comes when Jesus is willing to die on our behalf, for our sins, that we might have life forever.

If you think carefully about those closest to you, there is likely at least one person in your life that understands and practices what it means to show unconditional love toward others. These are not loud and noisy people clamoring for attention. Rather, you'll find them quietly serving others right where they are. They aren't waiting for sometime in the future to make a difference; they are making a difference today.

What happens when unconditional love is introduced into the equation? Everything changes. Nothing stays the same. And no one can go back after they have experienced it, even just once.

Unconditional love heals the broken, empowers the timid, affirms the hesitant, and elevates those who have been over-looked, forgotten, and silenced. There is a power that comes to those who show and to those who receive unconditional love. Those who show this love are released from being consumed with themselves. Those who receive this love are released from limitations others have placed on them.

Unconditional love sets us free so that we might live according to God's plan for our lives. Further, it sets in motion the steps necessary to bring about the kingdom of God on earth while we wait for the coming of a new world where unconditional love will exist in its original form, without human manipulation or corruption.

Too often we excuse ourselves from opportunities to embody unconditional love because we are convinced we aren't smart enough, mature enough, experienced enough, or rich enough to make a significant impact. That simply isn't true. You have everything you need right now to show unconditional love toward someone else. This book is about ordinary people, just like you, who did extraordinary things when they released unconditional love in and through their lives.

God blessed what they were doing for others and enlarged their influence and impact. You can be part of that blessing, too. *Unconditional Love* is not a challenge for the future but now. It is not something we can wait to do but is something we must initiate right now.

You can be an agent of change. It will look different than what you might think. But there is great power in letting go of that which is holding us back. Choosing to recklessly share unconditional love with others in the same way God has done for us will change you and the people you reach.

As you read the stories of these courageous individuals, don't forget that each of them were, and are, just like you. They had, and have, the same fears, the same lack of resources, and the same limits you have. The difference is they trusted that unconditional love would multiply their efforts. They bet everything on what they were doing, and all of them have seen a significant and lasting return on their investment because they trusted God to work through them. The secret is out: unconditional love changes everything. These people changed the world, and YOU can, too.

Papa Joe Bradford

Elijah's Heart

P apa Joe Bradford has overcome poverty, discrimination, prison, and kidney disease. After being forced to move to the "projects" due to unavoidable financial hardship, Papa Joe and his wife, Denise, discovered children who were desperate for someone to love them and care for them. Music became the gateway to the hearts of the children they met and their broken families in this all-but-forgotten community.

Through Elijah's Heart, Papa Joe and Denise are able to continue their effort to reach underprivileged children and their families through music, provide for basic needs such as food, and become an advocate for a crowd of people so marginalized by society that they are often dismissed before ever being given a chance.

Papa Joe's Story

Papa Joe Bradford, like many African-Americans in the South during the 1960s, grew up poor. He reflected, "We were so poor we didn't have our own outhouse." But everyone around him was poor, so no one knew any different.

His father left his mother before he was born. Joe, his sister, and their mother lived with their grandmother. Living in a segregated community, Joe grew up watching two buses drive by his house on the way to school: one for white children and the other for African-American children. But Joe's mother was convinced that he needed to ride the bus with the white children to learn about the real world.

As time went on, Joe reached past the discomfort of feeling out of place. He eventually made friends and went on to earn the citizenship award in the eighth grade. Earning good grades became a primary focus for Joe. He knew he had the ability to do well in school and watched closely the habits and practices of other students who did well in the classroom.

Joe's love for music started early. He started playing an instrument in a school setting in the sixth grade. While he wanted to play the trumpet at first, a wise music teacher encouraged him to try the saxophone. Joe had a gift for music and went on to win awards and earn statewide recognition for his ability to play both the alto and tenor saxophones.

Martial arts were also part of Joe's life thanks to his grandmother's encouragement. She knew life would be difficult for Joe and wanted him to be able to defend himself if he ever needed to. This never replaced her emphasis on education. She would often tell Joe, "A man ain't nothin' without an education."

With both school and music, Joe was drawn to the discipline of practice. He learned he was very good at martial arts and often daydreamed, as many young boys do, of one day being a Samurai. Joe said, "I thought there was something in a Samurai that was the secret to being a hero."

Joe's high school years were filled with victory and accomplishments. He was the first African-American in his class to make the Beta Club, be elected as his graduating class's vice president, and sit on the student council. These experiences affirmed that a good attitude, hard work, and discipline could overcome just about anything that life may throw at you.

Given all his accomplishments both in and out of the classroom, Joe rightfully earned a full scholarship to the University of Tennessee to study engineering, one of the most demanding inter-disciplinary areas of study. While at the University of Tennessee, he worked around computers. At that time mainframes produced by IBM were available.

During those days people had to schedule time to work on a computer. Joe recognized the opportunity to learn about programming and technology through the on-campus work-study program. With discipline and commitment, he learned all that he could about computer technology. He knew this was an opportunity of a lifetime, and he wasn't going to miss out on it.

Part of Joe's drive was to prove to his dad, whom he did not know and who had not been part of his life, that he never should have left him. This unresolved pain was soothed by achievement and recognition Joe received from others. Joe's discipline and commitment were really attempts to mask the unresolved hurt, pain, and resentment of feeling abandoned.

On a dare from a fellow classmate, Joe used all his knowledge about computers, programming, and technology and hacked into a restricted banking system. Joe says, "It's the things that you accomplish that sometimes hurt you." Joe believed his success made him invincible. He was arrested and convicted, but the judge allowed him to finish his senior year of college. On graduation day Joe walked with his class to obtain his diploma, only, instead of walking into a corporate job, he had to appear before a judge for sentencing. "The judge made an example out of me," says Joe. He was given the maximum sentence under the law. The next segment of his life journey would be dark, but was a necessary catalyst for Joe's healing and experiencing a personal reset in life.

Being in the Knoxville jail during the 1980s was anything but comfortable. The prison was overcrowded, and Joe had to sleep on the floor for thirty days. Joe, as he had done before, eventually earned the attention of the leadership.

Joe became the most popular person in that particular jail. When the sheriff learned that Joe knew about computers, he asked him to help he and his staff learn how to use the newly installed ones in the jail. Joe even established a GED program for the inmates to earn a high school diploma.

He became a model inmate and was given the opportunity to earn a work-release. The only obstacle was that Joe would have to be moved to the prison system from the jail system. This step seemed harmless, so Joe agreed. Joe was transferred to a prison known for housing hardened criminals. In fact, he remembers seeing James Earl Ray, who was convicted of killing Dr. Martin Luther King Jr., during his time there. What he thought would be easy turned into a nightmare.

He was placed in the violent offenders section of the prison. Joe later learned that this was punishment for what his record stated as fighting a police officer. He says, "I didn't mean to hurt anybody. When they discovered what I had done and came to arrest me, I got scared and broke away from the police. I certainly didn't mean to harm anyone and didn't even know I had done so."

Joe quickly learned the rules of prison culture. He focused on survival and never backed away from the opportunity to defend himself, or others, when necessary. Eventually Joe could no longer avoid the inevitable. One of the primary bullies and his friends confronted Joe, who was trying to defend another prisoner. All of the pent-up rage was released in that moment. Joe not only defeated these men, he went after the bully himself. When he was finally pulled off the guy, he was not sure if the bully was even still alive. Joe knew he had lost control of himself.

He was given forty days in solitary confinement for his behavior. What was supposed to be a six-day visit turned into a much longer stay. It was during those forty days that Joe dealt with his anger about his father. He looked inward and recognized how he had gotten to this low point in his life. As many difficult circumstances often do, it was also the beginning of the healing process from all his anger that resulted from not understanding or accepting why his father did not love him and want to be in his life. "I was at the lowest point. There was only one direction left to go, and that was up," says Joe. He made peace with God and became a Christian. Joe emerged forty days later a new man.

After being released from prison, Joe had literally nothing but the clothes on his back. He lived at a half-way house for a while, often sleeping in different places, even at some of the homes of his fraternity brothers. Life seemed impossible.

Soon Joe would meet his wife, Denise, while at work. Denise had also come from a musical background. Her uncle played for Ray Charles for more than three decades. Denise was a spiritual woman who knew early in their relationship that God wanted them to get married.

Joe was afraid to tell her about his past because he didn't want to risk her rejecting him too. So he kept silent and avoided conversations that might have brought up the subject of his criminal past. But he knew that if their relationship was going to continue, he would have to tell her, but he wanted to postpone it for as long as he could.

Finally Joe realized he needed to tell her, yet she affirmed him rather than rejected him. This was confirmation for Joe that Denise was the woman of his dreams and the one he wanted to spend the rest of his life with. Within two and a half years of marriage, they had two small children.

On Joe's thirty-fifth birthday, he noticed his leg starting to swell. The doctors eventually discovered that Joe had a rare kidney disease. It wouldn't be long before he experienced kidney failure. Joe's diagnosis and condition resulted in dialysis treatment for nine hours a day, every day, for fifteen months. This led to a series of medical complications. Joe needed a kidney transplant, and he needed one soon.

While Joe was enduring his daily routine, he had time to read his Bible, pray, reflect on life, and discover more about himself and God. It was clear that God was using this time to prepare Joe for what was next. There was a resetting of values and importance when every day was a struggle for survival.

A kidney eventually became available. It was a match but the antigen number was low. This is the rating system that doctors use to predict the success rate. The outlook wasn't good, and there was no certainty that Joe would survive, given how weak he already was from his condition. But the doctors decided to go ahead with the procedure.

The good news is that the kidney procedure was a success. Joe's prayers and the prayers of his family had been answered. Yet the story wasn't positive on all fronts. Joe's dialysis had prevented him from working, which meant they had lost nearly everything they had in the process. There was no other option—he and his family would have to move to the "projects" and live in government-subsidized housing.

At first the complex didn't want to approve him because of his past. But thanks to a friend and a promise to start a choir for the children in the community, they were granted admission. Joe says, "I didn't know what God was doing at the time."

On the first day in their new home, a little girl around the age of ten showed up, and Denise gave her some candy. Joe was fearful of the expectation that had been set. He knew that one little girl would turn into many. Soon their home became a place where the children loved coming around. So many kids were playing in front of their home that it killed the grass. Some parents just dropped their kids off, knowing that they would be safe. Joe and Denise couldn't believe how fast these children learned who they were and felt comfortable and safe coming over.

Together, Joe and Denise started the children's choir they had promised the housing manager. About sixty children were preparing to sing for the National Day of Prayer event when one child, during a break in the practice session, asked Joe if he would be their daddy. Joe wasn't expecting that, but he also knew what was coming next. About thirty other children followed that one request. After all that Joe had been through, he realized his significance was to be a surrogate father to children who had no father and, for many reasons, little hope for a better future. From that day forward, Joe became "Papa Joe."

In 2005 Joe and Denise started Elijah's Heart as a way to expand their ministry to his community and invite more people to be part of caring for the children and the families within the community. Today the children's choir continues to grow strong.

In addition to music, Joe and Denise invited the community to be part of "A Walk of Love." This is an effort to distribute food to families who likely wouldn't have any without this program. "We've never not had enough food to distribute," says Joe. "Elijah's Heart has been blessed by the generosity of others."

Joe believes and puts into practice that God's command to love others can only be accomplished when we put love into action. "The Lord purposely puts us in positions where His glory will be revealed. I believe God sets us up, so He can prove Himself," says Joe. "The Bible teaches that the world will know Jesus' disciples by their love for others (John 15:13)."

If you could sum up the life philosophy of this man transformed by the grace of God into an instrument of peace, hope, and love, it would be this: Don't get angry. Don't judge. Just demonstrate God's love to others.

Discussion Questions

1. Papa Joe had to overcome a lot of personal challenges, but he never used them as an excuse to give up. What challenges are you facing today? Do you feel like giving up? Why or why not?

2. Financial hardship forced Papa Joe and his family into the projects. What unexpected twists and turns have you had to endure in your life? How have those obstacles shaped you?

3. Papa Joe and Denise recognized an opportunity to use their love and gifts of music to reach the hearts of the children in their community. What gifts has God given you that you could share with others? Are you using those gifts today?

4. Elijah's Heart provides for the practical needs of people in need. How can you leverage your abundance and excess to help others? Describe a time when someone helped you during a challenging time in your life.

5. Papa Joe has become an advocate for the poor. Who around you needs you to become an advocate for them? Who has been an advocate for you in your life at critical moments?

Contact Information

To learn more about this organization or to find out how you can help, please contact Elijah's Heart using the information below:

Web: www.elijahsheart.com
E-mail: contact@elijahsheart.com
Mailing Address:
2817 West End Avenue #126-272
Nashville, TN 37203

Helen Ashe and Ellen Turner

The Love Kitchen

elen Ashe and Ellen Turner are twin sisters who were taught to think about the needs of others from an early age. As nurses, they were frustrated by the injustice they saw while working with indigent patients. Helen often thought about how she could help the people no one else wanted to help. One day she had a dream to help the poor and indigent community in Knoxville, Tennessee. Her twin sister, Ellen, challenged her to do something about it. Together, in 1986, they opened The Love Kitchen and served twenty-two meals in the basement of a small church.

Today The Love Kitchen prepares and serves more than two thousand meals every week. More than 80 percent of those meals are hand-delivered to people who are unable to physically leave their homes. Helen and Ellen, both in their eighties now, still actively lead the effort they began more than twenty-five years ago. They want everyone to know they are loved, and there is hope for better days ahead.

Helen and Ellen's Story

Helen Ashe and Ellen Turner are twin sisters. They grew up in Abbeville, South Carolina, before segregation. John and Alice, their parents, worked hard, but there was little chance to rise above poverty for African-Americans living in the South in the 1930s, not to mention the Great Depression.

Segregation was a very difficult time if you were an African-American living in the South. Before entering the house of a white family, you had to take your shoes off, enter from the back door, and only eat after the white family had finished eating. There was a line that African-Americans didn't cross, and there were always rules to remind both races what expectations existed for each other. No other options existed except to go along with it.

Helen and Ellen lived in a small house in a very rural area. Their father worked in the fields while their mother worked in a private home. Life was hard, but Helen and Ellen always felt loved. "The things we had to go through were a blessing because of the parents we had," Helen says.

Their father had a third-grade education but taught himself to read the King James Version of the Bible through personal commitment and determination. Helen and Ellen never forgot this. Their dad would quote from the Bible often and was a very religious man. Once, when Helen and Ellen were

18

little girls, they decided to sample the food of all the men who would leave their lunchboxes in their home while they worked out in the field with their father. When lunch time came, the girls realized they were in trouble for eating other people's food. When lunch came and went, and no one said anything, they thought that no one noticed, but later that night they learned how important it was to respect other people and what they had. "We tried our best to blame it on our dog, Flick, but our parents didn't believe us," says Helen and Ellen.

Helen says, "Our father taught us three things: There is but one heavenly Father; there is but one race, the human race; never take the last piece of bread from the table because someone might come by and be hungry." These foundational truths have guided Helen and Ellen's decisions for their entire lives. From as early as they can remember, they were taught to be mindful of the needs of others even though they did not have much at all.

Segregation was hard, which meant little opportunity for their parents, but their parents hoped things would change and that their daughters would have more opportunities in the future. "Our parents were very talented and worked hard for what little we had," says Helen.

Helen and Ellen did attend school at the age of six and eventually graduated from high school. After graduation the two girls were told that their parents had saved some of their money to send them on a bus trip to visit family in Knoxville. They enjoyed Knoxville and the surrounding area so much that they never returned to South Carolina. Over time they worked in a cafeteria and even owned their own restaurant. They did almost everything together, just as they had done their entire lives.

One day they decided they wanted to become nurses, so after completing college, they started to work in a nearby hospital. Helen, in particular, worked closely with the patients of a clinic connected to the hospital. Many of these patients did not have health care. It was unlikely that they would be able to pay some or even all of the costs of the care they needed. "I would sometimes give them money to eat, ride the bus, or whatever their needs were," says Helen.

Helen and Ellen protected each other always. Helen became ill and was admitted as a patient to the hospital. When she was not treated with the same respect as the white patients, even though she had health insurance and was able to pay, Ellen challenged the hospital's treatment of Helen and even contacted some advocacy groups. Ellen's determination paid off because Helen ultimately received the treatment she deserved.

Each day Helen and Ellen rode the bus to and from work. Helen would always say to Ellen that one day she was going to do something to help the people who would come into the clinic. She wanted to do something meaningful to help these people who were often looked down upon because they didn't have a lot of material things. "These patients would come in and wait for hours to be seen. They didn't have any other chance at receiving the care they needed," says Helen.

Helen was inspired by Dr. Martin Luther King Jr.'s speech "I Have A Dream." She would often say, "Just like

Martin Luther King Jr., I have a dream. I need to do something about it." Ellen finally looked at her sister and asked when was she going to stop talking about doing something and get something done. So that's what they decided to do.

Helen and Ellen decided to open The Love Kitchen as a way to provide meals to people who were hungry. Their first day of operations was in the basement of a small church in February 1986. There were no commercial appliances, no large seating area, and no finances to begin their work. They simply just began. Helen and Ellen served twenty-two meals on that first day. "People thought we were crazy," Helen says.

Unfortunately they were not able to stay in the basement of that little church for long, but God provided a new place. "We had to move, but God provided a place for us quickly. We never missed a meal," says Helen. The amazing thing is that Helen and Ellen have never had to worry about food or supplies. The community has always been incredibly generous, and no one takes a salary at The Love Kitchen. Everyone is a volunteer, including Helen and Ellen. People show up at particular times to deliver food that is donated, prepare the meals, and serve them. Helen and Ellen continued to work as nurses until they retired, pulling double duty in the kitchen while caring for those that were sick at the clinic.

The Love Kitchen has grown a lot over the past twenty-five years. What started as twenty-two meals has evolved into more than two thousand every week. And more than 80 percent of those meals are hand-delivered to people in their homes. "So many people who need food can't leave their homes. Sometimes it's because they can't drive, and sometimes it's because their bodies won't let them," says Helen. The sisters work hard to keep variety in the menus, especially for the homebound, so they don't end up eating the same thing week after week.

If there is one thing that makes Helen and Ellen more upset than anything, it's when someone only eats a portion of their meal and then throws the rest away. "We know that good people donate food, and we were taught to eat everything on our plate. We try to tell them that God gave them this food to eat to stay healthy. He would want them to eat the whole thing," Helen says.

They love reading all the cards people send them. Sometimes they are from volunteers, sometimes they are from people they have helped over the years. Every once in a while, they receive a card from someone they know who is struggling, yet they have placed a dollar or two in their card to help. "We have some people who give a lot of money. But when someone gives a dollar or two and have it hard, we know that's the widow's gift. We know that gift has been bathed in prayer, and God will doing amazing things with it," says Helen.

The sisters are now in their eighties. They want to continue to operate The Love Kitchen as they have for almost three decades. Helen and Ellen pray constantly. "We find our strength in prayer," they say. "It would be impossible to go through all we do physically and expose ourselves to so much need emotionally without prayer," says Helen. Ellen has already had to fight cancer and was recently hospitalized due to sickness. The transition plan is still unclear, but the commitment of these two women to The Love Kitchen is nothing short of divine devotion. It is likely they will continue until their bodies no longer allow them to function. They believe that God gave them the dream to start The Love Kitchen, and He will continue to bless it as long as they are faithful.

After a recent generous donation, they will be able to build The Love Kitchen Community Center where they offer training classes. It will also serve as a safe place for underprivileged children. Helen's dream continues to evolve and unfold in ways that neither Helen nor Ellen could have predicted.

"Prayer is what keeps us going," they say. "We give food to people who need help. We want them to know they are loved, and they have hope," says Helen.

Discussion Questions

1. Helen and Ellen grew up in a time when the South was racially divided. How do you think that shaped their view of other people, particularly the poor? Has someone ever unfairly made assumptions about you? What happened? How did it make you feel?

2. Helen and Ellen began The Love Kitchen after seeing how harshly indigent patients were treated at the hospital where they worked as nurses. Remember a time when you observed injustice. How did it make you feel? Did you do anything about it? If so, what?

3. The Love Kitchen began in the basement of a small church; they didn't wait until all the details had been worked out. What's keeping you from helping someone else today? Why do we tend to wait for the big opportunities to help when there are small opportunities around us every day?

4. Helen and Ellen don't have to continue the work they began, but they do because it's who they are. What has God uniquely gifted you to do? Are you doing it? How is postponing obedience preventing you from experiencing God's blessing?

5. Helen and Ellen believe everyone needs hope and love. How are you helping others find hope and love? Describe an experience that stands out in your mind.

Contact Information

To learn more about this organization or to find out how you can help, please contact The Love Kitchen using the information below:

Web: www.thelovekitchen.org
E-mail: thelovekitchen@gmail.com
Phone: 865.546.3248
Mailing Address:
PO Box 6839
Knoxville, TN 37914

Magnus MacFarlane-Barrow

Mary's Meals

M agnus MacFarlane-Barrow had already been delivering aid around the world to people in need for nearly a decade when he stumbled into Malawi. While there, he met a mother dying from AIDS and her young children who would soon lose both parents to the horrible disease. This mother's prayer was for someone to look after her children after she died. Edward, her oldest son, told Magnus that the two things he hoped for were an education and food to eat.

That encounter in 2002 became the beginnings of what would become Magnus's life's work. Mary's Meals provides food for children within a place of education. What started in Malawi has now become a global endeavor. Today Mary's Meals coordinates with more than five hundred places of education in sixteen countries and serves meals to more than four hundred thousand children around the world.

Magnus's Story

Magnus MacFarlane-Barrow grew up in a family of seven in Argyll, a rural community in Scotland. Like most boys, he spent a lot of time outdoors. Magnus especially enjoyed hunting and fishing. Mangus's parents were devout Christians and faithful to bring up their children with a strong sense of faith and hospitality.

His parents ran a guesthouse that they eventually turned into a retreat center. "I never remember a time when we didn't share our living space with someone else," says Magnus. There always seemed to be someone who needed help or a safe place to stay because their life was in transition. Sometimes they would stay for a short time, and other times it was an extended stay. This had a profound effect on Magnus.

Magnus remembers the Bible story when Jesus and His disciples were trying to get some rest after ministering to the people, but their attempts were foiled when the crowd found them. The disciples were upset, but Jesus quickly started ministering to the people. "I think about this story when I think about my parents. They never tired of helping others, and they never held anything back," he says.

Magnus grew up to be a salmon farmer in the same community where he was raised. He lived a rather normal life, involved in church, but felt his faith was divided. Magnus said, "I was involved in church, but I put my Christian life in a nice, neat box. I didn't live a social life that was consistent with what I believed, and my friends were not open to things of faith."

The Bosnian conflict of the early 1990s captured the attention of Magnus and his brother, especially the images they had seen on TV of people suffering. "We both felt very moved by what we saw and wanted to do something, even if it was small, to help," he says. They decided to get the community involved in their efforts by collecting food, blankets, and clothing.

Magnus and his brother drove the supplies to Medjugorje in Bosnia and Herzegovina, a special place to them both because his family had visited the country as teenagers. They distributed the donations to the people in need, and upon their return Magnus thought everything would go back to normal. "I really thought I had done my good deed and could go on with the rest of my life," Magnus says. But the community donations kept pouring in, so he kept delivering them.

Eventually Magnus gave up his job, sold his house, and committed himself to driving aid back and forth. "I remember telling God on one of those trips that I would do this for as long as the donations continued. I had no idea this would turn into my life's work," he says.

Magnus continued to deliver donations and aid to places where wars, famine, and poverty prevented people from getting what they needed to survive. What started as a desire to do something to help turned into a ten-year endeavor. "I learned during this time that people, whether they claim to have faith or not, are generous. People want to help when they understand the need and are given the opportunity to help," he says.

There were plenty of times when Magnus thought he wouldn't be able to continue. He assumed the donations would eventually stop. He wondered where he would get the money to repair the van or pay for gas. "Every time I needed something, the provision just showed up. It seemed like a miracle every time," says Magnus.

One thing he learned, especially when delivering supplies, was to build good relationships with local partners. He says, "I became very good friends with the people I was working with, good trusting partnerships." This ensured his access to the area and his safety while he was there.

While delivering supplies to various places, he observed two different approaches in distributing humanitarian aid. One approach is to build relationships with local people to carry on the work while going back and forth delivering supplies. The other is when outside organizations just show up, drop supplies, distribute, and leave. Magnus believes that when someone else comes in and drops supplies without building relationships, they run the risk of patronizing the poor. "I may be the one delivering the supplies, but I never lose focus that everything I do is about the people who need the help I provide. I'm simply a way to get that to them. It's really not about me," he says.

Magnus was impressed with how easy it was for the poor to trust in God. "Spending time with the poorest of the poor has taught me what it means to live completely dependent on God," he says. Magnus thought he was the one helping the poor, but the poor helped him grow in his faith and his devotion to living the gospel story through his life.

His work eventually brought him to Malawi, Africa, in 2002. They were experiencing a very bad famine that year. Magnus had no idea that this place would give birth to his life's work. "I really stumbled into this community. I wasn't looking for it or to start anything new," he says.

While there he met a family devastated by HIV/AIDS. The father had already died of the disease, and the mother, Emma, was dying and in extreme pain. Magnus knew Emma wouldn't live much longer. She told him there was no hope for her, but she was deeply concerned for her children. Magnus says, "Emma told me, 'There is nothing left but to pray for someone to care for my children.'"

Magnus turned to her oldest son who was fourteen, whose name was Edward, asking him what his desire was for his own life. He says, "Edward looked at me and said, 'I want to be able to go to school and have food to eat.' My heart sank."

While Edward and his five siblings did not have the virus, they had very little hope because there was no food and no chance for them to get an education. "What most people don't know is that the very poorest children around the world never get the chance of an education because they have to go out searching for food or work while the parents go to work. This is how they survive," says Magnus.

He was struck by how simple the idea would be to provide a meal for every child within a place of education. Magnus knew that education and food would raise the people out of poverty around the world. In Malawi, things became very clear for Magnus.

That was the beginning of what would become Mary's Meals. Up to that point, Magnus's work was done under the name Scottish International Relief. "Mary is in reference to the mother of Jesus. She was a refugee and grew up in poverty," he says. So, Magnus officially changed the organization's name to Mary's Meals and began a new work in Malawi.

When he started, Magus called together the members of the community to explain what he wanted to do. He also wanted to get their permission. "We weren't going to get started without support from the community," Magnus says. "That was the only way this was going to work."

Everyone agreed, and the work began in one primary school. It didn't take long for children to show up for school who never had been or hadn't been to school in a long time. Soon, surrounding schools wanted to offer a similar program. They saw what was happening and wanted to do it in their school, too. Magnus saw the potential for this model to allow the program to expand. It seems he had stumbled onto something that worked and had the potential to have a profound impact. He says, "I still maintain Mary's Meals was an accident."

"At every step along the way, I never thought about what I was doing as my life's work. I just saw a need and responded to it," Magnus says. Up to this point, his relief and aid work had taken him all over the world to places like Romania, Bosnia, Croatia, and Liberia. The new work in Malawi quickly consumed most of his time. "We didn't immediately stop our work in other places, it just eventually faded away as we focused on Mary's Meals," says Magnus. He was committed to maintain some of the work he had been doing, especially continuing to support the children's homes he had built in Romania.

Magnus believed in what was taking place in Malawi. Apparently, others did too. It quickly caught on and gained momentum outside Malawi and the surrounding areas. "God took what we were doing and blessed it. I believe we are called to do small things. If God wants to bless small things and make them bigger, that's His decision," he says.

Magnus is constantly encouraged by the support Mary's Meals receives from people around the world. "We've experienced very little resistance, even from governments. If they don't officially support us, they are apathetic to what we do. But no one has ever prevented us from working in their country," he says. If Mary's Meals can provide a child a meal in a place where they receive an education, Magus believes these children have a real chance at rising above poverty later in life.

Today Mary's Meals operates with only forty full-time employees. They operate in more than sixteen countries and partner with more than five hundred school and child-care facilities. Mary's Meals feeds more than four hundred thousand children around the world. Ninety-three percent of every dollar donated goes directly to relief.

Magnus believes three things have made Mary's Meals successful: a broad army of volunteers, simplicity of vision, and unwavering devotion to the mission. There are more than sixty-five thousand volunteers in Malawi alone. "I have no idea how to even count the number of volunteers who support us in our work around the world," he says. The volunteers help bring in supplies, cook the meals, and feed the children. "There is no way we could have the impact we do without them. These are often local people who want to help the children in their own community."

The simplicity of the vision of Mary's Meals makes it easy to describe to others: to provide a child a meal in a place of education. "It's not difficult to understand or complicated to communicate," says Magnus. Magnus continues to be amazed by the generosity Mary's Meals receives from people all over the world who are not just feeding children but giving them a chance to have a better life than their parents.

"Wherever we go, we see so much need. It would be tempting to try to solve all of them," says Magnus. "It's easy to get distracted, so we have to stay fully devoted to our mission." He is convinced that Mary's Meals is called to accomplish something very specific. There are times when they do make an exception and feed children outside places of education, especially in places experiencing famine, but it's rare.

Mary's Meals works; it's a simple concept that gets results. Magnus has seen children thrive in the classroom who previously did not have access to food or an education. It has transformed communities and given hope to people who otherwise would not have any reason to believe their circumstances would change. This is another important reason Magnus believes he has been able to gain support. He says, "People used to think I was crazy to have such a lofty goal. Now they think it's crazy that children can't have one meal every day in a place of education."

Magnus doesn't think he is doing anything spectacular, but he knows that Mary's Meals is making a difference in and around the world. Magnus says, "All I'm called to do are the things in front of me. If my starting point is to do something outstanding, I'll almost always fail. The small things are enough. God will do the rest."

Discussion Questions

1. Magnus grew up in a family that believed showing hospitality toward others was important. He never remembers a time when his home wasn't shared with someone else. How do you think growing up like that helped him be sensitive to the needs of others? Define hospitality. What role does it play in the Christian life?

2. Magnus recognized the need of the Bosnian people and wanted to do something about it. He started collecting donations of food and clothing and delivering it to Bosnia.

When were you so moved by the needs of others that you did something to help? How did you help? What do you remember most about that experience?

3. Magnus never thought of Mary's Meals as his life's work until much later. Why is life always clearer looking back than ahead? Is there something in your life today that began as something very small? What has surprised you the most along the way?

4. Mary's Meals is very focused in its effort: provide meals for children within a place of education. Why is staying focused essential to achieving impact? What advantage does clarity about the work we are called to do and the people we are called to help give us? Explain.

5. Magnus believes we change the world by doing small things for other people. What small things can we do today to improve life for someone else? Name one person you can show kindness to today. What's keeping you from acting on that desire right now?

Contact Information

To learn more about this organization or to find out how you can help, please contact Mary's Meals using the information on the next page:

Web: www.marysmeals.org
E-mail: info@marysmealsusa.org
Phone: 1.800.385.4983
Mailing Address:
590 Bloomfield Avenue
Unit #280
Bloomfield, NJ 07003

John Croyle

Big Oak Ranch

J ohn Croyle was an all-American defensive end who played on the 1973 championship team at the University of Alabama coached by the legendary "Bear" Bryant. There was nothing holding him back from playing professional football, that is, except his heart. After an encounter with a child in New Orleans, he committed his life to build a place where children could be cared for, loved, and finally feel safe.

At the age of twenty-three, John established Big Oak Ranch and became the father to five orphaned boys. Nearly three decades later more than eighteen hundred children have found a place they can call home and a family they can call their own. John has no regrets about leaving football behind and has built a legacy of unconditional love into the lives of the next generation.

John's Story

John Croyle was born and raised in Alabama. The oldest of two children, he remembers a normal, happy childhood surrounded with love, laughter, and full of life. That is, until the unexpected happened.

He and his little sister were attending the funeral of an extended family member. As little children often do, they found themselves innocently playing without any concern or awareness of danger. No one had any idea they were in danger nor could anyone have predicted what would happen next. John and his sister were skipping across the top of headstones in the cemetery behind the church while everyone else was preoccupied inside. John heard his sister scream and so he looked behind him. A three-hundred-pound stone had fallen on top of his sister, and she wasn't moving. Later the doctors revealed that the stone had pushed two ribs into her heart and two into her lungs. She did not survive the accident.

John had no idea how to process such a tragic event. He felt a pain no child should have to experience that early in life. He admits there was no type of counseling that could ease the pain of watching your little sister turn blue and die. John said, "God doesn't kill children to make someone else tough. There must be a bigger plan." John's parents loved him and never blamed him for the accident.

This was a defining event in John's life, one that would always remind him just how precious life is and how much of a gift the people we love are to us and to others. But this experience was only one of many that would prepare John for the unique call God had on his life.

In ninth grade life seemed almost perfect. He was popular, a good student, and a great athlete. John's dad was offered a significant promotion, one that would double his salary. This would give them enough money to have the life that his dad had always dreamed of giving his family. The only catch was that taking the promotion meant uprooting the family and relocating to a different city. John's dad considered the implications of such a decision. Most important, he considered what it would do to John if he had to give up everything that was familiar to him with only a few years left before college. John remembers his dad rendering his decision to him. John said, "I'll never forget that conversation. My dad basically told me that he chose me and my happiness over a raise. That set an example for me that I've tried to live out in my own life and parenting." While John was grateful and relieved that they wouldn't have to move, he was also aware of what his dad was giving up. This was an example that John would not forget. Little did John, or his dad, know that he, too, would be asked to make a similar decision in the not-so-distant future.

Both John and his parents were active in their local church, although it wasn't until he was a junior in high school that he asked Jesus to come into his heart. He wasn't looking to be confronted by the gospel when he decided to attend a Campus Crusade for Christ meeting. He was, instead, looking for a pretty girl he was interested in dating when someone shared the gospel story with him. Later that night he prayed and asked Jesus to come into his heart.

Sports came naturally to John. He was all-American in football and basketball in high school. At the age of eighteen, he went to the University of Alabama to play for Coach Paul "Bear" Bryant. Only a few days into his freshman year, John was injured after performing a standard drill in practice. John said, "I tore every ligament but one." When they finally stood him up, he remembers his leg just hanging there. It was surreal. He quoted Romans 8:28 to himself: "We know that all things work together for the good of those who love God: those who are called according to His purpose."

John said, "This was the first time in my life when I had to work. Everything up to that point had come easy for me: friends, school, and of course, football."

He worked through the recovery by teaching himself how to do the simple things all over again. Failure was not a possibility and giving up was never an option. This resolve and passion would be the foundation of the strength he would need to be successful in what he discovered would be his true passion in life—children.

After observing a child in New Orleans who cared for his mom in a way that his mom should have cared for him, he dreamed about creating a place where children could feel safe, loved, and be given a real chance to succeed in life. He shared his thoughts with Coach Bryant. His advice was this, "Don't play pro football unless you are willing to marry it." John believes that this was his way of saying that if there is anything else in life that you'd rather do, then go do it. "Coach never said a lot, but he had his subtle ways of affirming my decision."

John finished school and subsequently walked away from every opportunity to play professional football. Many believed John was destined to be one of the greatest football players in history. When asked why not make millions and then start the Ranch, John simply says, "God wanted to make sure that no one else could get the credit but Himself. If I had earned millions from the NFL, people would have thought this is what John did." The Ranch, as time would tell, was John's calling, passion, and work.

At the age of twenty-three, John moved into a house with five other boys and started Big Oak Ranch. Purchasing the house was a miracle in and of itself and confirmed for John that God was going to provide and see this through if John would just be obedient to do what God had called him to do.

John's parents loved and supported him, though they were not without concern for their son. "I remember my dad being completely supportive. My mom, though, was worried about how I was going to pay for everything," said John. He reminds himself and others often, "God loves ignorance and can't stand arrogance."

It wasn't long before John found himself in the crosshairs with the Alabama State Department of Human Resources.

They came to the Ranch and demanded to see a license. John had no idea someone needed a license to do what he was doing. He actually got out his driver's license, thinking that was all he needed. The agent, obviously won over by John's blind courage, helped him understand the process and secure the proper state license.

There wasn't much money to go around in the early days. In fact, the only gift he could afford to give the five boys their first Christmas together was $20 each. And that seemed like more than enough. But money wasn't what John feared the most. "My greatest fear was messing a kid up instead of helping him," says John. "I remember lying in bed at night and wondering if I would ever be able to make a difference in the lives of the kids living with me. I learned as time went by that the success or failure of a child was not up to me. My job is to give them the opportunity to make the right decision." He took comfort in that and never veered from such logic.

Failure was never an option for John even though his journey was not free of obstacles. One particular obstacle was an electric bill for only $98. He remembers looking at it and knowing he didn't have the money to pay the bill. John was also aware that if he didn't pay the bill, the electric company would shut off his power.

John did the only thing he knew to do. He prayed about it. And God answered his prayers in a miraculous way. When he went to the mailbox, he found five $20 bills in a white envelope. No name, no address, just marked for the Ranch.

John joyously paid the $98 bill and gladly took the $2 balance home.

These envelopes with five $20 bills would appear from time to time in John's mailbox. He would later learn that the benefactor was an old friend who supported what John was doing but never felt like he could do enough to make a significant difference. John says, "What he never knew was that his gift and his timing helped keep us alive."

God continued to do miracles through Big Oak Ranch. It grew and multiplied in ways that few, including John, could have ever dreamed and hoped for. During this time God brought his wife, Tee, back into his life. They had known each other as children, and even at one point of their lives, John dated her roommate but had never thought of Tee in a romantic way.

Then one day, as it often does, that all changed. John had been dating, and almost married, another girl until he realized that the relationship wasn't right. Once he and Tee started dating, they never stopped. Tee accepted John's passion for kids as her own, and they never looked back.

Big Oak Ranch accepts children who typically fall into four categories: orphaned, abused, neglected, or homeless. John says, "You'd think that all of these children come from destitute families, but I've watched millionaire parents drop their children off at the Ranch in their Mercedes and drive away."

John's philosophy is simple. He has four governing principles that are the basis of community at the Ranch:

We will love you; we will not lie to you; we will never leave you; and we have boundaries and expect you not to cross them. Amazingly, John notes, we've never had a situation we couldn't handle.

Perhaps one of the most astonishing things about the Ranch is that none of its $5.5 million budget comes from government assistance. The entire operation is privately funded. John says, "We have to raise about $15,000 a day to care for these kids. While the stakes are high, I sleep just fine at night because God has always, and will continue, to take care of us."

John recalls a speech that Coach Bryant would give before every football game. He would say, "Boys, in this game there are going to be four or five plays that will determine the outcome of this ball game." John believes the same is true about life. He carries this philosophy forward into how he cares for kids. Just because someone has had a bad past doesn't mean they can't have a great future. He acknowledges that many of these kids have had a past full of pain that no one should ever have to endure. John's faith tells him that God is bigger than our past and our pain. He says, "God is a master physician but not a plastic surgeon. We all have scars."

John and Tee raised two biological children while raising hundreds more. John's son went on to play professional football in Kansas City for five years after being the starting quarterback at his alma mater. John's daughter is learning the ropes of managing and leading the ministry of Big Oak Ranch as John and Tee begin their transition into a broader role of ministry through speaking and writing. John says, "If we don't plan for continued expansion, this will fail. It wasn't about me, and everything shouldn't rest on me."

Many people look to John for inspiration and clarity around their own life's calling and passion. John asks them a simple question: If you had one year left to live, would you still be doing what you're doing right now? John says, "I want to walk through the gates of heaven empty handed and tired . . . the kind of tired that comes from a good, hard day's work."

John learned at an early age that life is precious and not everything should be measured by money. When it was time to make critical decisions, he never worried about the consequences or the details. Rather, he desired to do what was right and consistent with what God had called him to do. With the same discipline and resolve that made him a successful athlete, John stayed focused on the task he had been given. The result of his effort is a ministry that is living out the gospel message, the Good News, for many children who were abandoned or rejected by the people who were supposed to love and care for them.

While some might think John gave up the opportunity of a lifetime, he looks back on his decision to walk away from professional football without any regrets. He says, "I didn't walk away from anything; I walked toward something. I may not have a Super Bowl ring, but I wouldn't change anything."

Discussion Questions

1. John experienced the pain of losing his sister early in life. What difficult experiences shaped your life growing up?

2. John's dad walked away from a significant promotion because he knew his son wouldn't have been happy. Would you be willing to do the same for your kids?

3. John gave up the opportunity to play professional football to start Big Oak Ranch. Would you have made the same decision if it had been your choice to make? Why or why not?

4. John and his wife, Tee, have shared their love with hundreds of kids for almost three decades. How are you sharing what God has given you with those in need around you?

5. John has no regrets about his life. Do you? Why or why not?

Contact Information

To learn more about this organization or to find out how you can help, please contact Big Oak Ranch using the information below:

Web: www.bigoak.org
E-mail: info@bigoak.org
Phone: 205.467.6226
Mailing Address:
PO Box 507
Springville, AL 35146

Twjuana "TJ" Williams

Maplewood High School

T
wjuana "TJ" Williams may be the most unlikely teacher you'll ever meet. She never considered teaching as a profession, given her love and passion for the auto industry. A college-educated mechanic, TJ translated what she learned about rebuilding and restoring cars in a professional setting into rebuilding and restoring the lives of her students in the classroom.

Through Maplewood High School's auto mechanics program, TJ sees an opportunity to help students in a community marked by poverty, gangs, and violence, by teaching them a trade and helping them to discover a path to a much different life from what many of them think is attainable. Never hesitant to give from her heart, wisdom, or wallet, TJ is proof that anything is possible, even in the most unlikely places.

TJ's Story

"Cars are my life," says Twjuana "TJ" Williams. As early as she can remember, TJ had a knack for putting things together, tearing them down, and then doing it all over again. Unlike some things we do as children, this interest never went away, continuing to grow and develop with age.

Growing up in a military family wasn't easy. TJ was born in Alaska and attended eleven different schools in twelve years. "My parents were serious people," says TJ. She knew that what they said was true, and she always expected them to follow through on what they said. TJ always knew she was loved and knew the security of a loving home even though the constant relocation was difficult. The discipline TJ learned at home would be instrumental in the work God would eventually call her to accomplish.

TJ graduated from Maplewood High School and went to Auto Diesel College. As a professional mechanic, she received training from Ford, General Motors, and Toyota. She was very successful and progressed quickly in her career. One day she decided to leave the corporate world to teach because of a very unique opportunity.

"Most people thought I was crazy to leave the corporate world," says TJ. She first went to East St. Louis to consult with a local college about their automotive program. After one week the president of the college was convinced that they needed TJ's leadership. "The president came to me and said name your price because we need you," says TJ.

For those not familiar with East St. Louis, TJ describes it as a community that has been down for so long, giving up on trying to come back. The most troubling part to her was not the poverty but the reality that grown men could only read at a fourth- or fifth-grade level. "We don't have to go to Africa to find poverty, we just need to visit East St. Louis," she said. "These people had no hope and no desire for something better."

TJ took the initiative to find people in the community who would donate their cars to the college for the auto mechanics department to repair. In addition, she wrote and was awarded a grant that allowed the college to pay students in the program while they learned. She called this "earn while you learn."

There was plenty of resistance in the beginning, but TJ was taught never to give up until your mission was accomplished. She recruited seventeen adult students, and all seventeen students went on to graduate from the college and were given one of the cars they helped repair. She told them, "You have everything you need to get out of this place and make a better life for yourself. If you don't, it's your decision."

After leaving the college, TJ returned to Nashville, Tennessee, to manage a chain of auto stores, but that would not last for long. The principal of Maplewood High School, her Alma Mater, called to see if she was interested in returning to the classroom. "I wasn't looking for the opportunity, but I accepted the offer," said TJ.

Maplewood High School and the surrounding neighborhood had changed since TJ attended the school. It was a minority population that had little education and opportunity. There was a lot of crime in the area and many of the students who attended the high school were involved in gangs. Few homes had both a father and a mother in the home. Often, a grandmother, who was too elderly to really care for the children, was the guardian. They would accept custody to avoid the children falling into Child Protective Services or foster care.

The condition of the automotive program at Maplewood reminded her of where she had started in East St. Louis. "There was a lot of promise but a long way to go," says TJ. She knew she had a long road ahead of her, but she desperately wanted to make a difference. With limited budgets, supplies, tools, and no cars to work on, TJ rebuilt the program from the ground up with support from the community. "When I arrived, the conditions of the classroom were not conducive for learning. I had a lot of work to do before school began," says TJ.

TJ quickly assessed that the mind-set of Maplewood was that there was little hope for something better than what was right in front of them. "Many people believed and accepted that this was as good as it would get, and no one was pushing for anything else," she said. She was not willing to accept this and believed she could create an environment to overcome this pervasive mind-set.

Her first order of business was to bring some discipline to the classroom. TJ demanded that everyone would get along in the classroom, even if they were part of a rival gang. She had to create a safe environment where these students would focus on learning with the hope of a better future.

One puzzling recurring experience was the number of students who came to school and immediately put their heads on their desk. She couldn't figure it out, so one day she asked the question, "Why would you come to school and then go right to sleep?" TJ was not prepared for the answer she received. One student told her that the only reason he came to school was to eat because there was no food in his house. He explained that his dad was in prison, and he never saw his mother. His only hope of eating was to come to school. That's when TJ realized how much these students had to overcome in their personal lives, which explained why they were so disinterested in learning. She says, "How can I expect them to learn when they're hungry?"

From that day forward she started feeding her students. Of course, there was no budget money to cover this expense, so TJ decided to pay for all the food out of her own pocket. Already taking a much smaller salary than what she did in the corporate world, she never complained about the personal sacrifice. To TJ, it was the only logical thing to do. "I decided that it was more important to feed my 175 or so students every weekday than it was to buy things," says TJ. "I gave up on doing extras for me because I wanted to help them."

Every other day TJ goes to Walmart to shop for food. "If I can feed them, I can teach them," she said. In addition to food, TJ was able to secure a grant through the Urban League of Middle Tennessee where she leads efforts around workforce development. This grant gives Maplewood the ability to offer paid internships to help keep these students focused on learning and not feeling the need to rob someone for food money. "Sometimes these students feel like they have to rob a store or a person just to survive. These are things students, kids, shouldn't have to deal with but they do," she said.

But food wasn't the only challenge TJ would face. Over time she began to recognize that some of her students came to school with the same clothes on day after day. And many times these clothes would not be washed or cleaned before they were worn again. TJ, again out of her own pocket, purchased a washer and dryer for the shop. "It's not exactly what you expect to find in an automotive lab, but it certainly is essential to creating a healthy learning environment, especially for these students," says TJ. When a student's clothes need to be replaced but TJ realizes they don't have the funds to do so, she will buy them new clothes to wear.

While access to food and clothes helped, some students couldn't help but get into trouble. It might be that they ran with the wrong crowd; it might be that they felt the need to rob someone to help pay for things around the house; or it might be that they felt the need to rob someone simply because they are bored with nothing else to do. For those students TJ started giving out her personal cell phone number with instructions to call her before they made a criminal mistake. TJ's promise was that she would come and get them no matter how far she had to drive, whether or not it was day or night, during the school week or on the weekend. She knew that many of her students didn't have another adult to lean on. They were forced to become adults even though they were still kids. And when her students call, she answers.

To no surprise of anyone who knows TJ, she has never accepted "no" as an answer. When a need presents itself, she finds a way to cover it. "Somehow, someway the details seem to work themselves out," she said. If the shop needs an upgrade or if the students need automotive uniforms, someone in the community always steps up or the funds become available. "Most people don't have because they don't ask," said TJ.

Many teachers find it impossible to teach at a high school like Maplewood. "These students need someone who is not afraid to die and willing to act with some little street smarts," she says. "If you hold them accountable and don't give up, they will come back to you." TJ knows her students need much more than what a classroom can provide, and she holds nothing back when it comes to helping those in need. She said, "Once you put the ingredients in the cake, you have to take the cake to the oven to watch it rise."

At graduation, she gives about eight or nine cars away to graduating seniors who need them the most. "These students either need the cars to get to work or have some other hardship," says TJ. In addition to the car, TJ extends to them the offer to bring the car back to be repaired at any point in the future. To her knowledge, all of her students still have their cars, and the vehicles are in running condition. "Only one student has traded the car they received through the program, and from what I know he wishes he hadn't," she said.

One of the most difficult experiences that TJ would have to face would happen outside the classroom. When her mom became deathly ill, TJ went to care for her. Dealing with her death was the most difficult thing she has ever had to deal with. She wasn't sure if she would return to the classroom, but before her mom died, she told TJ to make sure she went back to those kids because they needed her. "My students prayed for me during one of the darkest times I've ever experienced in my life. They prayed together and kept the spirit of our work alive while I was taking care of my mom," said TJ. "The truth is, my students saved me."

She says, "If God's will is a car, I want to be the wheel. I never want to get in the way of what God is doing." TJ knows it takes a lot of people to raise a child, but she believes the investment is worth it and will pay off in the future. She never holds anything back, and her students know that.

TJ feels good about the decisions she has made in life even though they have cost her in many ways. "I feel good about the choices I've made. This is the group of people I have been called to serve," she says. "It makes my soul happy to know that I'm giving all that I've got. I'm not holding anything back. I don't believe my work is in vain, and I'm confident God will continue to bless what's happening at Maplewood High School."

Discussion Questions

1. TJ had a successful career in the automobile industry before accepting the opportunity to be a high school teacher. Has God ever called you to take a step in a direction that some might consider a step back rather than a step forward? If yes, what did you do? If no, would you be willing to take a step back in your career if God asked you to?

2. Maplewood High School is located in a very economically depressed area. Nevertheless, TJ has helped these students acquire the skills, pride, and determination they need to rise above their circumstances. Have you risen above your circumstances? How did you do it? If you had the opportunity to help someone else do the same, would you? Have you? If so, what happened?

3. The students TJ teaches often have very complicated home lives. She gives beyond the classroom because she believes in these students and wants to help. In what ways have you personally sacrificed to help someone beyond what was expected of you? Describe your experience. How did it make you feel?

4. TJ describes her work at Maplewood High School as her ministry and passion. Can you do the same? Does your job match your passion? If no, how are you pursuing the call God has placed on your life?

5. TJ loves new cars but has never regretted giving up a corporate salary to teach. She says, "I don't have anything to prove to anybody." What in your life do you have or do because you want to prove to others you are successful? How is that getting in the way of God using you to help others?

Contact Information

To learn more about Ms. Williams or to find out how you can help, please contact her using the information below:

Web: www.maplewoodhs.mnps.org
E-mail: twjuana.williams@mnps.org
Phone: 615.262.6770 ext. 1217
Mailing Address:
Maplewood High School
401 Walton Lane
Nashville, TN 37216

Jena Nardella

Blood:Water Mission

J ena Nardella first encountered injustice through a homeless man on the streets of San Francisco at the age of nine. She couldn't finish her meal knowing he was hungry, so she and her mom went looking for the man they had met earlier in the day. They never found him, but she never forgot him. That single encounter altered the rest of her life.

While still in college, Jena met the Christian rock band Jars of Clay and heard about their ideas around a new effort God had placed on their hearts called Blood:Water Mission. She couldn't stop thinking about it, so she took the initiative to put together a twenty-five-page strategic plan for the band to consider. Jars of Clay loved her ideas and asked her to join them and turn her ideas into a movement. Today,

Blood:Water Mission provides life-saving water and health care for more than six hundred thousand people in thirteen countries around the world.

Jena's Story

Jena Nardella grew up in a wealthy suburb of San Francisco with her mom, dad, and younger brother. She and her mom were walking the streets of downtown San Francisco one day when she encountered a homeless man for the first time, who told her he was hungry and hadn't eaten in days. Jena was confused and startled all at the same time. She says, "At the age of nine, I had no context for this, and I didn't understand why this man was hungry and didn't have at least one person who could care for him."

Having lunch later that day, Jena tried to finish her meal but couldn't. Her mom knew she was bothered by the whole experience. She suggested Jena ask for a take-out box, so they could both go looking for the man and give him something to eat. They never found him, but Jena never stopped thinking about him. "I love that my mom was willing to help me look for him. She affirmed me in that moment," she says.

Jena and her family moved to Colorado Springs several years later. By the age of thirteen, she found herself bored at church and decided to sneak out to spend time with homeless people in a local park. "I thought church was boring, and I was intrigued by the people I met in the park," Jena says.

High school brought many new opportunities for Jena to feed her passion to serve the hungry, homeless, and forgotten.

There was a Red Cross shelter nearby where she ended up working as the kitchen facilitator. Jena says, "My family was very understanding in that they would allow me to miss a lot of family time so I could pursue the things that I was passionate about." Many days she would finish school and go straight to the homeless shelter.

Jena attended Whitworth University in Spokane, Washington. She went to college with the intentions of becoming a nurse just like her mom. The first two years of undergraduate study were in the classroom, which is where Jena excelled. When it came time to begin clinical rotations, she discovered that she didn't quite have the stomach to handle all the things nurses encounter on a daily basis. She says, "I kept passing out at the sight of blood and didn't handle many ailments very well. I couldn't stand being sick all the time."

She was devastated by not being able to pursue something she really wanted to do. At the time Jena didn't want to think about doing anything else, but it seemed she didn't have a choice. "Everything in me wanted to make it work, but God didn't design me to be a nurse."

Jena decided to take another route—political science. During this time Jena was exposed to information about the HIV/AIDS epidemic and found herself captivated by all the conversations taking place among political figures, non-profits, and celebrities in hopes of drawing attention to this global pandemic. AIDS and HIV were still very controversial subjects, and few evangelical churches or organizations were giving much attention to the issue.

"The AIDS virus is scary. No one dies from AIDS. It shuts down your immune system. Sicknesses that most people can recover from kill people with AIDS," says Jena. She learned how difficult it was for people in the United States to cope with HIV and AIDS. Jena couldn't imagine what it must be like in places around the world where there was no access to healthcare, sanitary conditions, or clean water.

"HIV attacks the weakest part of the body. It also attacks the weakest people around the world," she says. This was an important metaphor that connected her experience with the homeless man at the age of nine with the complex global issue she was learning about. What Jena realized was that she didn't just have a passion for people with HIV/AIDS or homeless people, she had a passion for people who were overlooked and marginalized.

Jena was given the opportunity to speak at a conference at Grand Canyon University in the fall of 2003 about global injustice, particularly the HIV/AIDS pandemic. It was there that she met and impressed Steve Garber from The Washington Institute. Little did she know he was also talking with the Christian rock band Jars of Clay about ways to connect their faith with social action.

One year earlier Dan Haseltine, lead singer for the band, went to Africa to put names and faces with the statistics he had been hearing related to the HIV/AIDS epidemic. Dan was so moved by what he observed. People lived at a level of poverty he didn't even know existed. He wanted to do something about it, but he didn't know what to do.

Dan scribbled on the back of a napkin the words "Blood:Water Mission" while flying back home. He was meditating about Jesus dying on the cross and the water and blood flowing from His side when the soldier pierced His body with a spear. Dan thought that image was a perfect metaphor to describe what he had seen and the way it made him feel.

Two months after Jena's presentation (in November of 2003) to Grand Canyon University, Steve arranged for Jena to meet with the band members of Jars of Clay after a concert. Both Jena, Dan, and the rest of the band felt an immediate connection. They knew they were seeing the world through similar eyes. "It was a great evening full of great conversation, great ideas, and lots of passion," says Jena. "What was missing was a plan."

Jena couldn't stop thinking about how to make Blood:Water Mission function and accomplish what Dan had hoped for from the beginning. She took a chance and wrote a twenty-five-page proposal that outlined how Jars of Clay could launch Blood:Water Mission. With a little help from her dad, she felt good about what she had written down. Unsure how it would be received by the band, she sent it to them anyway. "My dad encouraged me to send it to them and take a chance on what might happen," she said.

The band loved her proposal. (Today they refer to it as "the manifesto.") They contacted Jena and asked her to leave er home and join them in launching Blood:Water Mission. Of course Jena said yes. "Jars of Clay took a big risk with a twenty-one-year-old. It didn't make any sense, but I've learned God shines the brightest when situations and circumstances don't make sense," says Jena.

Blood:Water Mission started with $1,000, most of that going to legal fees to set up a formal nonprofit corporation. "I lived in the basement of Dan's parents' home, I had a makeshift office in a local church, and my college computer," says Jena. "That's where this organization started."

The early days were tough. Jena often questioned whether or not she had made the right decision to move. The most formidable obstacle that Jena and Jars of Clay had to overcome was fund-raising. "No one had done much of it, and no one was really excited about doing it," says Jena.

In addition to limited funds, Jena made regular trips to Africa to establish partnerships and to get the work moving forward by herself. "It's no small thing to start a nonprofit organization. It takes a lot more than just passion and a great idea," says Jena. "I had no idea I would be spending most of my time on things like strategic planning, administration, and operations." She struggled with the responsibilities of her role because she wanted to be doing the work instead of leading the work. Jena recognized that without a strong, healthy organization, Blood:Water Mission would not be able to sustain itself as it grew. One person who helped Jena immensely during this time was her dad. "He helped me apply strategic planning and management to all the different moving pieces.

There was a period of time when a day didn't go by that I didn't talk to my dad," she says.

Jena was surprised at the number of organizations already on the ground in Africa working on the issue of HIV/AIDS. What troubled her was that many of them seemed to miss the point. "I realized that many others were so focused on their numbers that they missed the people they were trying to help," she says. "Organizations and programs can sometimes hurt more than they help when people aren't kept at the center of the work itself."

Blood:Water Mission wants to accomplish its work by leveraging relationships with indigenous partners. This is their long-term plan. Jena believes local leadership has the best chance of sustaining any relief effort. That means Blood:Water Mission must keep its focus on equipping and supporting local leaders. "Our approach is a very different model from what many organizations seem to do," she says.

Jena believes the concept of *neighbor*, especially in identifying who we are responsible for, is changing. She says, "People in Africa are our neighbors." That's why Blood:Water Mission focuses on more than just addressing the symptoms of HIV/AIDS. Jena wants to be part of the prevention of it, too. Blood:Water Mission focuses on providing clean water, health care for infected patients, and teaching good hygiene habits. "There is a strong connection between the spread of the disease and things like clean water and good hygiene. While we can't eliminate HIV/AIDS, we can slow the rate at which it spreads, and we can help those with HIV/AIDS live long and full lives," says Jena.

One mother and widow whose husband died of AIDS and is herself HIV positive, is alive today because of the work of Blood:Water Mission. The good news is that her children are not infected with the virus. However, due to a bad case of tuberculosis, she only has one lung. Because Blood:Water Mission was able to bring healthcare, hygiene education, and clean water to her village, this widow and mother is now helping others in some significant ways. She now helps other members of her village learn things like good hand-washing techniques, how to dig pit latrines, and develop a general understanding of how diseases are spread. "In a community where 24 percent of the people are HIV positive, this woman is saving lives while we are saving hers," says Jena. "An added benefit is that because this woman is HIV positive, she opens the door for people who are unsure or quiet about their status."

Another woman that has been helped through the work of Blood:Water Mission is now part of a soap-making business. Jena says, "This woman is using what we taught her to provide soap for the village. By selling the soap, she generates enough money to support her family." Sustainable change is not just treating the problem but offering people, who otherwise wouldn't have the opportunity, the ability to dramatically improve the quality of their lives and the lives of their families.

Jena believes change is created in small increments. She says, "Don't wait for the grand moment to make a difference. It starts today." Jena also encourages others to see the uniqueness of their own story. "It's likely that God has already used you to make a tremendous difference in someone's life," she says. She often challenges other people to find the "twenty-five-page manifesto" within them that is waiting to be expressed and connect with a real opportunity for impact.

"We are not called to save the world. Jesus has already done that. We are, however, called to serve the world. When we follow God and serve others, there is joy," says Jena.

Discussion Questions

1. Jena's first encounter with a homeless man on the streets of San Francisco at the age of nine made a lasting impact on her. Describe a similar experience you've had. How old were you? What happened? In what ways did that experience shape you?

2. Jena was passionate enough about helping others that she looked for opportunities to serve in the community. Have you ever been so passionate about a cause or charity that you intentionally looked for ways you could help? What did you do? List three things you learned while serving others.

3. Jena was in college when she first met Jars of Clay through a mutual friend. How has God orchestrated

encounters with just the right person at just the right time in your life? What came about as a result of those encounters?

4. Jars of Clay didn't ask Jena for a strategic plan. She took the initiative to put it together. Have you ever been so passionate about an idea or opportunity that you felt compelled to act even if it failed? If so, what? How did things work out over time?

5. Jena believes we shouldn't wait for the "big moment" to start following God and serving others. What's holding you back from following God's call today? How can you serve someone today and show them unconditional love?

Contact Information

To learn more about this organization or to find out how you can help, please contact Blood:Water Mission using the information below:

Web: www.bloodwatermission.com
E-mail: bloodwater@bloodwatermission.com
Phone: 615.550.4296
Mailing Address:
PO Box 60381
Nashville, TN 37206

Mackenzie Bearup

Sheltering Books

M ackenzie Bearup was a normal, active ten-year-old girl until she was diagnosed with a rare disease— *Complex Regional Pain Syndrome.* The extreme pain caused by everyday tasks limited her ability to attend school, participate in sports, and even ride in the car. She discovered she could escape her debilitating pain by reading books.

After learning about a center for abused children near her home, she decided to start collecting books to fill their library in an attempt to share her love for reading and to provide a similar escape for children dealing with another type of pain, emotional pain. Since 2007 Sheltering Books has expanded its reach to more than twenty-five states and has collected and distributed more than 119,000 books to children dealing with homelessness, abuse, and neglect.

Mackenzie's Story

Mackenzie Bearup grew up in Alpharetta, Georgia, an active suburb of Atlanta, with her mom, dad, and two younger brothers. To look at her life from the outside, she seems like any normal nineteen-year-old, but her journey up to this point has been anything but ordinary.

At the age of ten, Mackenzie was diagnosed with a rare neurological disease called *Complex Regional Pain Syndrome*. It is also sometimes referred to as *Reflex Sympathetic Dystrophy*. One of the conditions from this disease is chronic pain that affects one or more of the extremities of the body. For Mackenzie, the debilitating pain was most intense around her left knee.

It wasn't a tragic accident that caused the onset of her condition. She was doing what other ten-year-old girls often do, jumping on the bed while watching an episode of her favorite television show. Something happened during this playtime that was unexpected—intense pain. It seemed to occur almost instantly. Unfortunately this was the beginning of a condition that she has to live with for the rest of her life.

The type of pain Mackenzie endures on a daily basis is most commonly brought on by vibrations or touch. Something as simple as hitting a speed bump while riding in a car can trigger the pain and bring her to tears. It also became difficult to attend school because of the risk of walking down the hallway between classes and accidently bumping into someone. Of course, this pain also meant no sports, cheerleading, or dance teams were in her future.

Mackenzie's diagnosis wasn't made immediately. Like many who have rare conditions, it took parading in front of multiple physicians before one was able to accurately identify the cause of the pain. Several doctors she went to see were convinced that it was simply a sprain or some type of stress fracture. Eventually a doctor connected her symptoms with the rare disease. This was the first time someone could explain what was going on with Mackenzie and why the other treatment regimens weren't working. It was a relief to the Bearup family to finally be able to name the cause of her unusual pain.

Even after a formal diagnosis was made, it was a struggle to describe her condition to friends and peers in a way that they understood its intensity and severity. Most people thought she was just making it up to get out of doing what she didn't want to do. Mackenzie's middle school gym teacher gave her a failing grade one year because she refused to dress out during class. No amount of explanation could satisfy her coach. In addition, other students and teachers didn't completely accept what she was going through and often dismissed her episodes of pain as over dramatic and unnecessary. When the pain hit, Mackenzie would almost certainly buckle under the pain and begin crying.

Mackenzie said, "It was difficult at times because no one seemed to understand what I was going through, and they didn't want to believe me." Her parents eventually came to the conclusion that they would need to homeschool their daughter for her physical and emotional safety.

Countless therapy sessions have helped Mackenzie cope with the pain. She says, "I may not be able to do everything, but I can do many things." This positive outlook on life is one reason why she didn't choose to allow her condition to limit her ability or willingness to make a difference.

In addition to physical therapy, Mackenzie takes Ketamine infusions through an IV as part of managing her pain. Each treatment spans three days and lasts five hours each day. This occurs every other month and physically wipes Mackenzie out.

One of the ways that Mackenzie has learned to pass the time during her treatments is reading books. She had always liked reading. Mackenzie quickly realized that she could get lost in a story and forgot about the pain and the lifestyle that went with it, even for just a few hours.

She says, "Using reading as therapy is something that can take you away from everything." Mackenzie describes how getting lost in the story makes her feel normal again.

Mackenzie's discovery made her wonder if she might be able to help others experience a similar relief by providing books and encouraging them to read. Her intuition would definitely lead her to take some significant steps. However, it wasn't without the influence of some special people in her life who showed her what was possible even when everyone else said it was impossible.

While some might think it would be a stretch for a fourteen-year-old to think so deeply about life, the seeds of her desire to help others were planted in her early in life. She vividly remembers visiting her grandfather who was a double amputee and struggled with severe arthritis. He always seemed to find the strength and energy to help others and never complained about his condition. Her grandmother had her own battle to fight with her body. She was diagnosed with multiple sclerosis. As she got older, her grandmother's care became more intense. Mackenzie remembers her grandfather faithfully caring for her grandmother in spite of his limited physical capabilities until the day he died.

There were signs early in Mackenzie's life that she was destined to do something significant to help others. At three years old she asked her Mom for money to buy toys for other kids instead of candy for her own Easter basket. And during one visit to her grandparents around age eleven, she saw a local news story about a battered woman's shelter who needed shoes. She, along with her parents, went door-to-door and collected more than two hundred shoes in one weekend. What many would see as a problem too big for one person to solve, Mackenzie believed she could do something to help.

Given all that she had previously done to help others, it is really no surprise that Mackenzie decided to respond in a similar way when she learned about a nearby center for children who had been severely abused and had no place else to go. She says, "I saw kids who had been beaten, thrown through windows, and abused in ways that I had never even thought was possible." Mackenzie remembered thinking that these kids were dealing with pain just like she does, only this pain was on the inside.

She recognized that the on-site library for this residential community was lacking in its selection of books. She decided to start collecting books to fill the library so that the kids could find a similar escape through reading. It had greatly helped her, and she hoped it would do the same for them.

Her effort started slow but eventually gained momentum. Each time Mackenzie would return to the facility with more and more books, she was rewarded with seeing the faces of happy and excited children. It thrilled her to know that she was helping them find some peace and comfort in their troubled lives. Mackenzie remembers one little boy in particular she encountered. He seemed like a genius and obviously read all the time, just like she did. She remembers him being polite and well-mannered. As she talked to him, he explained that he had been abused as a foster child and had learned to use books as a way to escape. She says, "You could see the pain in his eyes." He personally thanked her for providing the books for their library. That was a conversation she'll never forget.

Mackenzie started asking friends and neighbors to donate books and help her pass out flyers. She asked anyone and everyone to help her spread the word about what she was trying to do. The result was nothing short of a miracle. Within twelve months, Mackenzie had collected more than eleven thousand books. The facility was running out of room for the books she was donating. They encouraged Mackenzie to start looking for other places that might benefit from her love of reading and knack for collecting books.

"It was in that moment when I realized there might be something to this idea of reading therapy," says Mackenzie, "so I started looking for other places to donate books." One option that she hadn't considered was homeless shelters, particularly those who helped families with children. She started contacting them and distributing books to these families. For many of these children, this was the very first book they could call their own. She loves personally giving the books away because she can see the excitement in the eyes of the children.

Soon, other opportunities began emerging. Around back-to-school time, she started giving away books at an event where these same children receive backpacks, school supplies, and other necessities for the coming school year. These are children who otherwise wouldn't have these things.

Her parents have always been very encouraging. They have never discouraged her and gladly opened up their home and garage to store the inventory of books she receives from all over the country. Known locally as "the book girl," Mackenzie has earned a reputation that transcends her physical condition, just like her grandfather had done during his life.

So what do Mackenize's friends think about all of this? "My friends treat me as normal, but there is also a recognition that something is different. People see that good things happen when you do nice things for other people," she says. Mackenzie tries to involve her friends as much as they are willing. Her family continues to help her expand her effort.

Mackenzie's mom is officially the Chief Executive Officer of Sheltering Books. In fact, it was her mom who submitted the initial application to CNN (cable network) that nominated Mackenzie for the 2010 CNN Hero Award. Mackenzie wondered if life could get any better.

Out of all the submissions from across the country, CNN chose twenty-two to be considered finalists for the CNN Hero of the Year Award. Mackenzie remembers a film crew coming to her house and transforming their living room into a studio. She was one of the youngest to be chosen as a finalist in the history of the award and was elated with the opportunity to share her story and the mission of Sheltering Books with the entire world.

Today, Sheltering Books has expanded into more than twenty-five states and has distributed more than 119,000 books. Her passion is perhaps even stronger today for what she is doing than it was when she first started.

One of the most challenging realities of running Sheltering Books is the cost of mailing books. "People don't realize that a box of books can cost as much as $50 or more to ship," says Mackenzie. "It's expensive, which limits my ability to distribute books." She notes that it costs as much as $10,000 or more to ship books around the country in a single year.

Mackenzie's dream for Sheltering Books seems to be ever-expanding. "We want to be in every state and distribute more than one million books," says Mackenzie. She wants Sheltering Books to be a household name.

In addition to collecting and distributing books, Mackenzie has started sharing her life story with others through public speaking. Whether it's at Girl Scout meetings, book clubs, churches, or schools, she is ready to share her story with others in hopes of encouraging others to push through what holds them back and look for ways to make a difference. Already managing twenty speaking engagements a year, she expects this area of her work to continue to expand.

Anyone with chronic pain struggles with the question, "Why me?" Mackenzie, however, chooses to use her condition as a reminder of how many others experience pain, emotional or physical, and have yet to discover a way to escape. This keeps her moving forward, even when her body tells her to slow down.

When asked what advice she has for others who want to make a difference with their life, she says, "Be as tough as you can. And never give up." She wants everyone to know that they have the ability to make a difference in the life of someone else if they will see their disability or pain as an opportunity to reach out and help someone else.

Mackenzie says, "There will always be someone who has experienced more pain than I have. I want to help them find the relief I have found through reading books."

Discussion Questions

1. If you were Mackenzie, would chronic pain hold you back or propel you forward? Give an example of how this has played out in your life.

2. Why do you think it was possible for Mackenzie to use her disability as an opportunity to help others? What is holding you back from helping others?

3. Have you ever experienced something that others refused to accept or understand? How did that make you feel? Does it make you more sensitive to the needs of others?

4. How important is it for Mackenzie's family to support her? Do you support the passions, dreams, and desires of the people in your family?

5. What can we learn from the example of Mackenzie's grandfather? Describe someone in your life who has provided a similar example.

Contact Information

To learn more about this organization or to find out how you can help, please contact Sheltering Books using the information on the next page:

Web: www.shelteringbooks.org
E-mail: mackenziebearup@shelteringbooks.org
Phone: 678.427.1316
Mailing Address:
Sheltering Books, Inc.
11877 Douglas Road
Suite 102214
Alpharetta, GA 30005

Diane Latiker

Kids Off the Block

D iane Latiker lives in a part of Chicago known for gangs, criminal activity, and poverty. What began as a desire to connect with the friends of her youngest daughter has become a community-wide effort to invest in young people and give them an alternative to the daily violence. Diane, a mother of eight and married for nearly three decades, has become the surrogate mother of her dangerous inner-city neighborhood and is making a difference that will impact generations.

Kids Off the Block provides a safe place for young people to make different choices in life, choices very different from what the streets offer. Education, sports, music, and personal respect are among the things championed by Kids Off the Block. More than fifteen hundred young people have benefited from this nonprofit community program that began in the home of its founder.

Diane's Story

Diane Latiker is a one-of-a-kind woman who has become a champion of young people in a neighborhood that offers few alternatives to lifestyles that lead to criminal activity, poverty, addiction, and death. "I live in a place that most people in Chicago don't even know exists," she says. Diane explains that there are four public high schools that serve the kids in her neighborhood, but only 4 percent of high school juniors are performing to state standards. "This is a place you only hear about when a child dies in a senseless shooting," says Diane.

One of six children, she remembers her mom being a significant influence in her life. "My mom always believed in each of us and thought we could conquer the world," says Diane. She didn't think much about it at the time, but her mom's words, encouragement, and prayers would be answered in a way they never could have anticipated.

Diane grew up, got married, and started building a family of her own. "I met my husband after I noticed his hair. We winked at each other, and with the help of my cousin who was with me, we exchanged numbers and started dating," she says. Nearly three decades later Diane and her husband are still married. Together they've raised eight children—four boys and four girls.

In addition to being a mom, Diane was a hairdresser, although, she admits that it was just a "job." She enjoyed the work, but it wasn't something that she was passionate about. "My mom opened a beauty shop for me and my sisters. I couldn't exactly turn her down," says Diane.

When her youngest daughter was the only child left at home, around the age of thirteen, Diane noticed that she was beginning to rebel and drift away. She had watched the activity on the streets of the neighborhood where she lived become increasingly more intense and deadly. Diane was determined not to lose connection with her daughter.

Diane prayed about what she should do to stay connected to her, and she decided that she needed to get to know her daughter's friends and start becoming involved in their lives, too. Diane remembered that she was always a leader in her youth group at church, and her mom would tell her that she had a gift for speaking into the lives of young people. As most children do, she brushed aside what her mom suggested, but she never forgot it.

All of these memories rushed back as Diane found herself, once again, with the desire to speak into the lives of the young people. One day she went outside and invited her daughter and their friends to come into her home, and they accepted. This was the beginning of what would later become Kids Off the Block.

Diane's youngest daughter was opposed to this outreach. She says, "My daughter wanted me to be her mom, not everyone else's mom. I respected her feelings, but it didn't hold me back." Eventually her daughter would accept Diane's ministry.

Diane didn't have a special program she followed. She didn't spend weeks consulting with others on strategy and direction. In fact, she never even considered some of the organizational obstacles she might face. This was simply a way to stay connected to her daughter and perhaps encourage some of her friends in the process.

Word quickly spread. Diane would invite not only young people but also their parents so they could see for themselves what the ministry was about. She understood how important it was to have parent involvement. Sometimes Diane found herself speaking into the lives of the parents as often as the young people. She realized the young people she was trying to reach were not just dealing with the realities of the streets; they were also having issues at school and at home. Diane would help these young people with their homework, encourage them to explore music, and provided opportunities to play sports such as basketball. It was a safe environment where these kids could be themselves and explore things that no one had ever encouraged them to do. "I have raised eight children, and these kids were teaching me things I had no idea about," says Diane.

The small group of friends quickly became twenty, thirty, and then fifty young people. Before moving into a new facility, Diane had as many as seventy-five young people in her home at a time. She was never scared for her life or felt like she was putting her daughter or her family at risk. While some of her older children didn't share in Diane's enthusiasm in the beginning, Diane knows they were looking out for her and trying to protect her from the unknown that might come into their home and bring harm to their mother.

"They were right to be afraid for me. In the beginning we had a brick thrown through our window and had a van shot up. This was all a message from gang leaders who knew members of rival gangs were working together," says Diane. She anticipated some resistance. It never occurred to her that stopping what she had started was an option, no matter what opposition she faced.

In spite of a few unnerving moments, Diane has never feared for her life or had to deal with unruliness in her home. "These kids respected me, knew they were in a safe place, and respected each other," says Diane. There were three rules that Diane had in place: no cursing; no use of the "n" word; and everyone had to get along. "It was amazing to watch kids who were rivals on the streets quickly leave all that behind when they were in my home," she says.

Few people understand the realities of living in an area like the south side of Chicago. The typical home has four to five children, and rarely has a dad in the picture. The family is likely to struggle financially, and because there is no money to afford daycare while the mother works outside the home, the oldest children end up doing most of the babysitting. The result for the oldest children is they miss a lot of school. They can miss so much school that they fall behind in reading and math. Eventually they drop out because they are embarrassed by how far behind they are in their classroom skills.

Most of the children in this neighborhood will have an encounter with the Juvenile Justice System before they are eighteen. With a lack of role models and limited opportunity, they turn to gangs who provide some sense of stability and family. For some, it's the only family they have and will ever know. Many of these children will not live beyond their twenty-fifth birthday.

Diane knew that if she was going to really change the life of a young person, it had to be done in cooperation with the parents. In the beginning there was some resistance, but most parents are grateful for what Diane has done and what Kids Off the Block provides for their children. She constantly reminds the children how important it is to respect and listen to their parents. "I often hear from parents how their child has changed in their attitude at home as a result of the time they spend with Kids Off the Block. This is no accident," says Diane.

One child in particular who stands out in Diane's mind that benefited from Kids Off the Block is a young man named Jerald. He was eighteen years old when Diane met him. The kids already in the program were afraid of him. Based on what they had told her, Diane was a little afraid of him, too. Jerald came one night to talk to Diane, and they ended up talking for more than two hours. She challenged him to change his life. "I told him he was a natural leader, but he was having a negative influence on others in the neighborhood," says Diane. She encouraged him to think about what he could accomplish if he changed his approach and started influencing kids in a positive way.

He listened, and he did change his ways. Later he told Diane that she had saved his life. He explained that the night they talked was the same night he intended to kill someone. He was on his way over to shoot a member of a rival gang. In fact, he had the gun he was going to use on him while they were talking. Diane was completely unaware of this. Jerald told Diane that he took her at her word and decided to go home instead.

"I couldn't be more proud of him. He is now in college. When not in class or at work, he spends his time on the streets influencing kids in a positive way. He has completely turned his life around," says Diane. This is the typical story you'll hear from those involved in Kids Off the Block.

God has certainly blessed Diane's efforts. She was invited to speak to African-American students at Harvard University. "I was so proud of all the African-American students who have made good choices that put them in the position they were in. Some of those were just like kids in Kids Off the Block and grew up in neighborhoods just like mine," she says.

She was also invited by the Prince of Dubai to participate in a Festival of Ideas. This included eighty leaders from all over the world and included twenty Nobel Peace Prize winners. Diane never imagined that a simple act of love and hospitality toward her daughter's friends would lead her to such a place of influence.

In spite of all the attention, Diane maintains a humble spirit. "There is so much more to be done. There are still people killing each other. No one wants to hear how simple the solution is. We all must come together and care about the people who live around us. It really does take a village to raise a child," she says.

After a young man died protecting a young girl in a shooting, Diane decided to build a public memorial in his honor. Every brick has the name of a young person who has died in a street shooting since this tragic event. More than two hundred bricks make up this memorial and sadly has been rebuilt more than a half dozen times. "We're always six to seven stones behind," she says.

If money wasn't an object, Diane would buy two vans and write, "I want to help you" on the sides of both. She would drive them around the neighborhood, pick up young people, and bring them back to the center that now serves as the central location for Kids Off the Block. "I want to help them do what is right; I want to help them make different, better choices for their lives," says Diane.

Diane takes no salary nor does any of her staff. "We do this because we love it. This is what I want to do with my life," she says. Diane believes that young people have a lot to teach adults if we will listen.

When people ask her about how they can make a difference, Diane encourages them to start where they are. "Look in your own community and discover what needs exist. Then decide to do something about it," she says.

Change happens when someone chooses to speak up, stand up, and step up. That's what Diane is doing through Kids Off the Block. She can't save everyone, but she can save some. She can't do everything, but she can do something. She can't reach every young person at risk, but she can reach as many as she can. And that's exactly what Diane intends to do.

Discussion Questions

1. Diane knew that one important way to stay connected to her children was by knowing their friends. How do the people we spend time with influence us? What do our friends say about us?

2. Diane started Kids Off the Block in her home. Would you be willing to open your home to others in need? Why or why not? If you have done so, describe your experience.

3. Kids Off the Block has saved lives by providing an alternative to what Diane's neighborhood has to offer young people. This has given these young people choices. How has your life been shaped by the choices you made? Name at least two people who have helped you see options you didn't know existed, or thought were possible, at the time. What impact has this had on your life?

4. Diane isn't paralyzed by the overwhelming nature of what she wants to accomplish. Rather, she is moved to take action. Recall a time when you attempted to do something

that was impossible or that others discouraged you from doing. What happened? What did you learn?

5. Diane has had the opportunity to speak all over the world about her work with Kids Off the Block. How has God multiplied your efforts to reach out and help someone? Identify one experience when this happened. How did it make you feel? What did you learn about God, about the person you helped, and about yourself?

Contact Information

To learn more about this organization or to find out how you can help, please contact Kids Off the Block using the information below:

Web: www.kobchicago.org
E-mail: diane.latiker@sbcglobal.net
Phone: 773.981.4077
Mailing Address:
11627 S. Michigan Avenue
Chicago, IL 60628

Linda Leathers

The Next Door

L inda Leathers never considered leaving her church staff position to start an independent nonprofit organization. But while doing some research to assess the needs within her community, she uncovered the unmet needs of women who are released from prison and have no place to go for help and were often forced into destructive habits to survive.

The Next Door offers hope to women who are incarcerated or struggling with addiction, abuse, or mental illness. Through this organization women are able to find the strength and confidence they need to create healthy, stable, and productive lifestyles. Many of these women are able to start over, and some are even reunited with their families as a result of their experience at The Next Door. Linda Leathers believes if you can change the life of a woman, then you can change an entire generation.

Linda's Story

Linda Leathers grew up attending church in her mother's womb in Florence, Alabama. "My mother is the godliest woman I know," she says. Linda watched her mother faithfully practice her faith through every area of her life in spite of her dad's lack of interest in spiritual things.

"I accepted Christ as my Savior at a young age. God has directed my path since then," says Linda. Linda started her career in Florida, working in sales and marketing for a computer science company. She attended Southside Baptist Church, which became a very special place for her. During her time there, she felt God calling her to shift her career direction and make a move into full-time church ministry.

She left life as she knew it to attend Southwestern Baptist Theological Seminary in her late twenties. "I never envisioned that for myself," says Linda. "What God did during that time was open my eyes to minister to single adults, which was an area of ministry I was aware of but had never really sensed the need or desire to focus on."

After serving two churches, she found herself on the ministry staff at First Baptist Church in Nashville, Tennessee. She had confirmed that her true calling and passion was local church and community ministry. At least Linda was convinced that God had completely revealed her life's work to her. But as God sometimes does, He called Linda to a new task, one that she never anticipated or expected.

While Linda was working at First Baptist, the church made several land acquisitions. One of those acquisitions included a building that stood on the adjacent property. The building was in an unusable condition, so the church could not decide what to do with it. Nevertheless, being a downtown church, they recognized that land is scarce and they needed to act on this opportunity for future ministry opportunities. It was during this time that Linda started to feel restless. She, along with a small group of women, started praying about how they could make a difference in the Nashville community. She says, "We called ourselves 'the wild group of praying women.'" This group that started with four women quickly grew to twelve, and eventually became more than one hundred women praying about how they could make a difference. Linda recognized that God was about to do something special.

This prayer group decided to start surveying the community to better understand the needs and how they might be able to make a difference. Linda says, "We were clueless, and we knew it. We had to do community research because we didn't know where to begin."

After speaking with more than forty organizations already working in the Nashville community, which included the head of Metro Social Services, Linda discovered a need that no one was addressing. "We discovered one huge gap that led to a wealth of untapped potential and unmet need," says Linda. Ninety-eight percent of women incarcerated today will be released. In Nashville, these women had no place to go to help them transition back into society. Many would simply return to what was familiar to them because there was no family support system to help them learn how to make different decisions. They had to return to drugs and the streets to survive.

Linda says, "God gave us a vision when we landed on that idea. We didn't know how we were going to address the need. What we believed was that whom God calls, He also prepares."

A few of the "wild group of praying women" decided to meet with the warden of the local jail. He was very kind to them but strongly discouraged them from trying to tackle this issue. Linda didn't believe he was trying to be rude or mean. She says, "He told us that we were just a bunch of 'do-gooders' and had no idea the type of people these women were." She'll never forget their conversation. He told her that prison was not the place for a kind group of church women. It was just too messy.

Linda believes, "If you can change the life of a woman, you can change an entire generation." Linda never accepted that these women were lost causes. God had given Linda freedom through Christ, and He wanted to do the same for these women, too.

During a tour of the jail, Linda observed how they release women after their sentence, literally raising a door and sending these women on their way. Linda wrestled with a growing desire to specifically help these women and captured it in a simple thought: "I want to be the next door these women walk through."

Linda's dream was to build a safe place for these women to live, have access to skills training, and integrate them back into society successfully. She says, "My heart broke when I realized there was no place for these women to do this in Nashville."

Linda also realized that she had no unique training that would prepare her to take on a task this big. She went to her pastor and talked to him about leasing the building and starting a nonprofit called "The Next Door" that helped incarcerated women prepare for life on the outside and helped those recently released to have the opportunity to change the direction of their lives. Linda says, "This building was just sitting there on the church property. It was screaming for a purpose."

The decision for the use of the building had to go to the church for a vote. While the pastor supported the idea, church structure didn't allow him the discretion to make this decision on his own. Linda prepared for this because she wanted to help the church understand the ministry opportunity they had uncovered. It was a huge risk, and it was very likely the church would say no. "It was a stretch to ask a large church to lease an old building to a brand new 501c3 led by a woman who had no unique or special experience in helping incarcerated women turn their lives around," says Linda. "To top it off, we had no money to offer the church. We needed a miracle to take place."

God did provide the building, which was already zoned to be used in this way, and through a capital campaign, the church was able to pay off the building and the land, giving it to The Next Door.

Linda didn't know until later, but there was already an elderly woman at the church who had been going to the jail and ministering to women. "No one knew it until she told us," says Linda. She was overwhelmed at how God had already been laying the groundwork for The Next Door, way before Linda even sensed God's call to move in that direction. It was confirmation for Linda that this was God's plan and not hers.

"We opened in May 2004 with one paid staff person and an amazing number of volunteers," says Linda. "We had been praying and preparing for this day. Now it was here." Linda did extensive research prior to opening to develop the right programming that allowed for conversations related to faith but also provided the very best results and outcomes.

One of the realities of this mission that Linda didn't expect is that once you open your doors and hearts to these women, it's 24/7. "There is no on/off switch," says Linda. She admits that it was their ignorance that allowed them to take this step of faith. Linda is convinced that if they really knew all they were getting in, they likely would never have done it.

It didn't take long for The Next Door to build a solid reputation with corrections professionals and the women they wanted to help. Linda quickly realized that she wasn't that much different from the women in the program. She says, "If I had gone through some of their circumstances, who is to say that I wouldn't have made some of the same decision." Linda recognizes that she lived a relatively sheltered life. "I didn't even know women went to prison before starting the work at The Next Door," says Linda.

One thing Linda remembers early on was that the women anticipating release and who were being interviewed for the program thought that you had to be Baptist to be part of the program. Linda laughs, "As you can imagine, there were a lot of Baptist women in Nashville's correctional system."

There is no faith requirement to be part of the program, nor is there any coercive approach to faith. Linda thought one staff member captured their approach best when she described it as layering Jesus into everything they do. "Our goal is total life transformation. While we don't push our faith on anyone, you can't help but bump into that conversation when you're dealing with things like anger, fear, and addiction," says Linda. The Next Door wants every woman to know that freedom is possible, that abundant life is possible, and there is hope for a better tomorrow. Linda says, "We want people to come to The Next Door to be healed. They come broken, and we want them to leave whole."

For Linda, one inspirational woman is named Ramie. Linda remembers that Ramie had a terrible addiction to crack cocaine. Ramie's daughter, a high school senior at the time, pleaded with her to be clean for her high school graduation. Ramie was arrested and placed in jail. After serving her sentence, she was placed at The Next Door. Ramie wanted to get clean and now she had the time to think through her next steps and evaluate her life. After a couple of months in the program, Ramie achieved sobriety and attended her daughter's graduation. Today Ramie is a part of The Next Door's staff and her daughter went on to Vanderbilt University, working for The Next Door while in graduate school.

The Next Door has services inside and outside the prison system. They provide continual services for women in risk or in crisis. Linda says, "The women who fall into this category are already incarcerated or likely to be given the right conditions."

While serving women in transition from incarceration remains their primary focus, they have expanded their reach to include women suffering from abuse and addiction. They have a housing community for women and children, which on any given day, there are about one hundred sixty women at The Next Door.

Since 2004 more than one thousand women have come through the doors of the Nashville facility. Linda says, "If they stayed one day or for the entire six-month program, they experienced respect, faith, and encouragement. Some were ready and some weren't. We can't control that. What we can control is that we were ready, open, and showed them love."

The Next Door desperately needs more room and more facilities. They simply can't keep up with the demand. "We never want to give up our commitment to doing things with excellence," says Linda. "And we always want to be sensitive to God's direction."

The Next Door believes the women they serve desperately need an opportunity to see and experience God's grace. Linda says, "These women are not bad people. They just made a series of bad decisions. Our place is not to judge. We just want to trust the Lord and run like crazy in the direction He is calling us."

Linda says, "I'm living a dream. I can't wait to see what God does next through the women, volunteers, and staff at The Next Door."

Discussion Questions

1. Linda believes women help shape society and culture in significant ways. Identify at least one important woman in your life. What role did that person play in your life, and how has that shaped you into the person you are today?

2. Linda had a comfortable job at a large church where she was already helping people. Why do *you* think she was willing to give that up? Is there something that you need to leave behind to be open to what God is calling you to do next?

3. The Next Door exists to serve women who likely have no family support system to help them transition back to healthy and productive lives. What would your life be like without your friends and family? Give one example of a time when you needed the help of others to get through a difficult

situation. How would the situation have been different if you didn't have anyone to lean on?

4. The warden told Linda and her friends that trying to help women in prison was too big of a problem for them to take on themselves. Why do you think God calls us to go places that we can't handle on our own? Have you ever been discouraged from making a big life decision by someone? Explain.

5. Our lives are the result of the choices we have made. We are all only a few decisions from being the people whom The Next Door seeks to serve. List three things in your life that contributed to your ability to make good life choices. How can you help other people around you learn how to make good decisions, too?

Contact Information

To learn more about this organization or to find out how you can help, please contact The Next Door using the information below:

Web: www.thenextdoor.org
E-mail: info@thenextdoor.org
Phone: 615.251.8805
Mailing Address:
PO Box 23336
Nashville, TN 37202

Faith Coleman

Flagler County Free Clinic

F aith Coleman knows what it's like to face a major medical event with no health insurance. Being a nurse practitioner, she completely understood the implications of being diagnosed with kidney cancer. Faith's treatment plan forced her to borrow against the equity in her house to cover the costs of the treatment.

During her remission, Faith found a new lease on life and started the Flagler County Free Clinic, a local, free health-care clinic that provides medical care to more than sixty-seven hundred people in her community. All of her patients are uninsured and meet the federal poverty guidelines. Faith was given the chance to beat cancer. She never wants someone to suffer or not have access to medical care simply because they are uninsured and can't afford the out-of-pocket expenses.

Faith's Story

Faith Coleman grew up one of six children, one boy and five girls, in rural Alabama. There were twenty-two people in her high school graduating class. Her mom was the rock and foundation of their home. Faith says, "My mom gave me my name because she wanted me to have a name I had to work at."

She was raised in a religious environment and exposed to things of faith at an early age. Her grandmother taught her the value of believing in what you were passionate about and hard work to achieve whatever that was. "She would tell me that if I did those two things, then the details would work themselves out," says Faith.

Faith's grandmother had a crippling case of Rheumatoid Arthritis. She never remembers her grandmother giving in or giving up even though just about everything was a struggle for her. Faith's grandmother kept going and never complained. She found strength in her grandmother's example.

Life has not always been easy for Faith. She remembers being in nursing school, pregnant with one of her children, and not having medical insurance. She did have access to minimal health care through government-funded Medicaid, but she was reminded often what stigma came with not having private insurance. Faith says, "I didn't mind being treated like I was poor. I was. But I didn't like being treated as if I was stupid. I wasn't."

Faith often reminds people that not having health insurance is not always a matter of choice. Sometimes circumstances don't allow an individual or family the ability to have private insurance. For those without it, the medical system can be tough to navigate, especially when you need treatment.

She began her nursing career in intensive care, where tragedy was normal. The pace was quick. It was an environment that came with pride when a patient's life was saved and sorrow when the patient died. Sometimes the line between life and death seemed too real, for everyone involved.

"It was one crisis after another," said Faith. She knew she didn't want to work intensive care for her entire career. Faith went on to become a nurse practitioner, and her goal was to help prevent people from ever finding themselves in need of any kind of intensive care.

"I've always believed that many of the difficult situations people face medically could have been prevented with the right preventative treatment plan," says Faith. Sadly, many people never receive preventative care and are forced to manage one medical crisis after another. In that situation no one wins, not the hospital, not the insurance company, and certainly not the patient.

In an unexpected twist of fate, Faith found herself in need of medical attention. She was diagnosed with kidney cancer in 2003, and, like so many others, she never saw it coming. But it was a new beginning for her; she just didn't know it.

The practical reality was that while Faith was a nurse practitioner, she was unable to afford health insurance premiums required to carry private insurance. The treatment she needed was truly either life or death for her, but she had no idea where she was going to come up with the $35,000 to cover the cost of the treatment. She didn't have that kind of cash in her bank account, and, with no other option, she chose to mortgage the equity in her home to cover the cost of the treatments.

Thankfully her treatment was successful and about nine months after going into remission with kidney cancer, she co-founded with a local physician the Flagler County Free Clinic. "Like many people who have come through a difficult life-threatening experience, I felt like I had been given a second chance. The Holy Spirit kept nudging me, and I remember thinking how fortunate I was to have a house to mortgage. But what about so many who can't do that?" said Faith.

Flagler County was, prior to 2008, one of the fastest growing counties in the United States, but unemployment has been high since the economic recession began. Along with the loss of jobs, also came rising home foreclosures. This left many hardworking people out of work and even homeless. Of course, no job meant no access to health insurance.

"People with no medical insurance can usually pay for office visits out of their pocket. Where it gets impossible is when tests are needed and more advanced medical treatment is required," said Faith.

The free clinic is open four days a month: two Thursday evenings and two Saturday mornings. Faith sees her work at the clinic as her life's work even though it is in addition to her own private practice. It truly is her passion. She hopes one day she will be able to keep the clinic open full-time. For now, Faith serves the people of Flagler Country with excellence, just as she would anyone with private health insurance that sees her in her private practice.

On any given Thursday, the clinic will serve twenty to twenty-five patients in less than three hours. Even though the clinic doesn't open until 5:00 p.m. on Thursdays, patients will begin lining up around noon. On Saturdays, when patients begin lining up at the door around 3:00 a.m., she starts seeing them around 8:30 a.m. The staff will serve sixty to eighty patients on Saturdays in about four hours.

When Faith realized the lengths some individuals and families were willing to go to get medical treatment, she knew that this was an overwhelming reality for which so many in her own community struggled to find a solution. Without the clinic, they would have no other options for medical treatment. That is, until it was necessary to visit the local emergency room, and sometimes that's too late.

Faith says, "For many of the people we serve, we are their primary care option and have been since our opening more than eight years ago." Not having private health insurance is horrific, just like homelessness and hunger. For those who don't have insurance, they live day by day hoping they, as well as their children, don't get sick, hurt, or involved in an accident that might require medical treatment.

The list of services provided by the clinic is similar to what you might find in any primary care physician's office.

Faith has worked hard to make sure they have covered all necessary treatment. The clinic is able to serve people in the areas of ophthalmology, women's services, dermatology, cardiology, and physical therapy, just to name a few. In addition to the services at the clinic, Faith has helped establish a network of physicians and specialists in the area who will help care for patients with special needs. "We never want to be in a position where we develop a treatment plan where we also haven't figured out how to accomplish it, especially for those without private insurance," says Faith. Many of the physicians and specialists in the area are happy to help out. They even invite the clinic patients to come to their private offices when necessary.

Faith has become somewhat of an expert in dealing with providers and hospitals. These are not easy waters to navigate because no one communicates well with each other. Often the patient is caught in the middle. She functions as an advocate for her patients and helps them navigate the murky waters of medical claims, hospital bills, and general administration details. "I've created form letters for medications, tests, and the like. I invite those opposing my recommendations to challenge my assessment," says Faith.

This level of persistence often results in her patients getting the treatment they need to overcome whatever physical challenges they are facing. She would rather play this role for her patients than to ask them to navigate a system on their own that they can't begin to understand.

In spite of all the curveballs life has thrown at Faith, she maintains a sweet spirit and positive outlook. Faith says, "Even as bad as we think we have it, someone has it worse." She is reminded of this every time she comes to the clinic to work. Faith believes that when bad things happen, we must look for the blessing because they are going to come.

The most surprising thing about the work at the clinic is they have not had to advertise for patients, volunteers, or supplies. "It seems like whatever we need, we have access to it when we need it," says Faith. In the early days Faith placed signs around town, but it didn't take long for the word to get out.

She has never had to worry about not having enough medical providers or volunteers. Faith claims she has never had to make a rotation schedule. "We all believe in this place and have a desire to help," says Faith. In addition to the support of the medical community, other members of the community support the clinic in other ways. Volunteer groups come to coordinate details, work the front desk, and help out however they can. Many people will even choose to have gifts sent to the clinic instead of flowers upon the death of their loved ones.

Faith has been surprised at how often supplies are donated at just the right time. Many of the items needed are not general household goods. She used to worry when supply levels were low. Over time she has learned that God will provide what they need just in time. "We might get low on something and then a local hospital, doctor's office, or medical supply company will call and tell us they are bringing by supplies for us. Whatever they bring, it seems to be just what we need at that time," says Faith.

The most fulfilling part of her work at the clinic are the people she is able to help. Faith is even willing to give out her personal phone number to patients so they have someone to call "after hours" if needed. Surprisingly, none of her patients have ever abused this privilege.

Faith remembers one woman who came to the clinic after finding a lump in her breast. She was able to help her get the necessary tests. Through Faith's work and the help of the clinic, they discovered breast cancer early enough to do something about it. Today this same woman has opened an after-school program for children to give them an alternative to destructive lifestyles that often involve drugs and gangs.

Another sixty-three-year-old man was diagnosed with neck cancer. Faith was able to help him get the necessary treatment, and today he is healthy and active. Faith talks about the homemade goods he bakes and brings by the clinic on a regular basis just as a thank you for saving his life.

While many might think that the clinic might be an unsafe environment, Faith cannot remember one time when she feared for her life. She does admit that sometimes it gets a bit chaotic, but when someone in line seems to get unruly, the others self-police the situation and the tension dissipates quickly.

Unfortunately Faith's cancer did return during the fall of 2011. She went straight to the hospital and it was a scary situation. Faith says, "I knew that if it was my time, then it's my time. I can't control that." Her treatment, for now, has put her on the right track. Faith knows she still has work to do and plans to continue to do that until she has no more time on earth. She finds comfort in knowing that God did not give her a spirit of fear but one of love (2 Tim. 1:7). Faith says, "I think God gives us the strength to keep moving forward in spite of the obstacles we face."

Faith does not remember a day at the clinic when there are not new patients in the mix. She anticipates the demand to continue to grow. In fact, Faith and others write for grants as often as possible. The dream is to find enough funding for Faith to give up her private practice and keep the clinic open full-time. Faith describes what she hopes for in the future, "I hope we have to close because we have no more patients. I hope that everyone has health insurance and our system has been reconstructed in a way that everyone gets the necessary medical treatment . . . regardless."

Faith knows she is on a mission to help others, and her only regret is that it took fifty years for her to figure it out and start doing it. She says, "When you help one person, it multiplies. You don't believe it until you see it. And when you do, you're hooked."

Discussion Questions

1. Faith had to borrow against the equity in her house to cover the medical treatments necessary to fight her cancer. Have you or someone you know been forced to make a

difficult decision as a result of an unexpected medical event? Describe the situation.

2. Faith doesn't fit the profile of what many might consider to be the uninsured. Nevertheless, she couldn't afford health insurance. How do the assumptions we hold and the expectations we project on others affect our ability to recognize people in need and our ability to help?

3. Faith decided to start a free medical clinic for the uninsured. Has a challenging experience in your own life led you start something to help others? Explain.

4. Faith has never had to worry about volunteers or supplies; both are available when needed. How has God provided for you when you stepped out in obedience to follow His call?

5. This clinic has become a lifeline for people who have no place else to go for proper medical treatment other than the emergency room at the local hospital. How can we be a lifeline to someone else? Write down the names of three people you know who need help. Describe how you could help them today. What's keeping you from following through?

Contact Information

To learn more about this organization or to find out how you can help, please contact Flagler County Free Clinic using the information on the next page:

Web: www.flaglercountyfreeclinic.com
E-mail: info@flaglercountyfreeclinic.com
Phone: 386.437.3091
Mailing Address:
PO Box 863
Bunnell, FL 32110

Travis Gravette

Global Support Mission

A trip to Uganda during college turned out to be more than a once-in-a-lifetime trip around the world for Travis Gravette. In fact, it disrupted the rest of his life. Travis discovered his life's passion: to help change the reality of people with no hope for a better life. Through a relationship with a local leader named Faith, who had escaped the plight of many in Uganda but returned to help, Travis discovered that change was possible.

Global Support Mission works through indigenous leaders to implement sustainable change surrounding the issues of hunger, disease, and extreme poverty. Since 2004, Global Support Mission has built a medical clinic, vocational school, and preschool, and provided orphan care, subsidized health care, and education for thousands. In addition, Global

Support Mission utilizes micro-financing to empower everyday people with the ability to make a measurable difference through the Know. Think. Act. Initiative. Travis believes taking action is what moves people from sympathy to compassion and, ultimately, will change the world.

Travis's Story

Travis Gravette grew up in a military family. His dad was in the coast guard, which meant moving along the Gulf Coast while growing up. The benefit of not staying in one place gave him a great perspective. Travis learned to value diversity at a young age.

A mission trip to Mexico in high school forced Travis to confront the reality of orphans around the world. He says, "Stats are great, but they lack a human element." Travis realized it's easy to get stuck in how we live and never consider the struggles of others who aren't afforded the same level of affluence and choices that we have as Americans.

During a Christmas break in college, Travis decided to take a trip that would forever change the direction of his life. He initially wanted to go to Africa, but while doing some research on Google, he discovered a woman named Faith. Faith grew up in a village that to this day remains plagued by disease and poverty. When she grew up, she moved to a nearby metropolitan area, escaping the fate of so many in her village. On a visit home to see her parents, Faith became overwhelmed with the effects of AIDS and poverty on the people in her village. She was grateful that she was able to escape and make a better life for herself; however, she also felt a responsibility to return home and help. So, that's exactly what Faith did. She gave up any chance at making a better life for herself in the city and returned to her village. It was reading about her decision that inspired Travis to redirect his focus and interest to see what she was doing in her village in Uganda.

Travis got in contact with Faith and told her that he wanted to be a part of her ministry. He recognized there was an element of danger in his decision to leave America, head to Uganda, and meet someone he had only interacted with through the Web. Travis felt like his research and interactions with Faith gave him a sense of confidence in his decision. He says, "Faith's story was compelling and her work was making a difference. I really wanted to see it for myself." Not knowing what to expect when he got off the plane, Travis was quickly reminded that the way we live in America is very different from the way the rest of the world lives. Uganda looked nothing like America, especially the village he would call home for the next six weeks.

Travis decided not to stay in a place that catered to American tourists, but instead he decided to live with Faith, immersing himself in the lives of the people Faith was helping. He says, "These people still shower outside and don't have enough food to eat three meals a day." The devastation was beyond what he could comprehend. Travis says, "The problem is so overwhelming that it's tempting to just shut down." But there was something deep within that awareness that led him to explore solutions to the problems he had come face-to-face with.

Living with Faith gave Travis a front-row seat to the work she was doing and the extreme conditions in which these people lived. He says, "People often miss out on relationships because they are so focused on process."

During his initial six-week visit, he witnessed Faith meeting the everyday, practical needs of people who had no place else to turn. Travis decided that the best way to get involved was to partner with her. He says, "I was just a college student. I chose to work through Faith because I didn't know what else to do." He admits that he could have chosen to work independent of Faith, but she was so inspirational. "Her sacrifice was so real that I wanted to honor that." Travis wanted to walk alongside Faith and help her continue to be effective in doing the work she felt called to do.

That decision would later become the basis of a service model that has allowed Global Support Mission to expand quickly and viably. He recognizes that choosing to work through local, indigenous leaders has accelerated their work and expanded their impact faster and more cost effectively than if they had tried to do something on their own.

After his return to the States, Travis continued to stay in regular contact with Faith. He would send her money from time to time, returning during summers, staying three to four months at a time. He felt deeply connected to the work.

Travis really struggled to understand what God was calling him to do. Should he continue to go back to Uganda and help Faith? How would he ever be able to make a difference? Would all his efforts really matter? He never gave up on the dream and desire to make a sustainable difference around the world. One of Travis's favorite Bible verses is Matthew 25:40, "Whatever you did for one of the least of these . . . , you did for Me." He says, "When we serve others, we serve Christ." Travis wanted to make a lasting difference, but he didn't know what his next step would be.

With the best of intentions, Travis decided he would make a lot of money and then be able to help in ways beyond his current capacity, but in 2006 he felt God was calling him to help support and expand Faith's ministry to the people of Uganda. "I clearly felt God telling me that Faith needed my help now, not twenty years in the future or somewhere down the road." This excited and scared him all at the same time.

Travis admits he never intended to start a nonprofit. It certainly hadn't crossed his mind. He might have done something completely different if he had not had interaction with Faith. He knew that to really help Faith, he would need to establish an organization around the effort. It had to be more than just Travis and his passion and dreams.

But where would he get the money? Did anyone else share his vision? How would he do this when it was just him? He says, "Americans always think that money is the best solution to every problem." His international experiences showed him that getting involved and taking action is just as important as sending money. Further, he never could let go of the idea of work through indigenous leaders like Faith. He says, "It just made sense. Why start over from scratch when Faith was already making a difference." He believes that had he tried to go around Faith, they would have ended up needing someone like her anyway.

Travis's parents were very supportive of his decisions. They certainly had their reservations about his decision to create Global Support Mission. His parents, like most parents, just wanted assurance that he was safe, fed, and healthy. "My parents never let their fears prevent them from encouraging me to pursue what God had called me to do." That was surely a gift and an assurance that Travis's decision was the right one.

He had no idea what it meant to start a nonprofit. Travis remembers buying a book that helped him understand the basics of the process and what he needed to do next. He laughs when he talks about the early days. Travis says, "I had no idea what I was doing. I didn't know what '501c3' meant."

The first year was by far the most difficult. Travis remembers going to close a bank account and being told that there was no money in his account. It was hard to find money to purchase groceries and the basic necessities. He remembers asking God, "I know you called me to do this, but why would you put me in this position?"

One day a friend called and wanted to go to lunch to catch up and hear more about Global Support Mission. Travis was embarrassed that he didn't have the money to eat out, but his friend wouldn't take no for an answer. During lunch Travis was able to share about his work and all that he was doing to get things off the ground. Not only did his friend pay for his lunch, he wrote him a large check. He says, "He explicitly told me that I was to use this check to take care of my needs. What he didn't know was how desperately I needed that check."

Travis never remembers when God didn't provide for his needs. In fact, he was eventually able to purchase a house. With several roommates contributing rent money, Travis was able to pay the mortgage without paying any of his own money. He saw this as God's way of taking care of him.

One of the most difficult things Travis has had to learn was how to build a team to accomplish a singular vision. It's hard to keep one person moving in the same direction, let alone a group of people. Everyone brings their own ideas, vision, and passion to the table. Leading a team allows Travis to share his passion and invest in them. He says, "When you work closely with other people, you see the good, bad, and the ugly. Everything comes to light, especially when the pressure is on." Travis believes investing in the people is the only way to make it work.

The greatest temptation he and his team have is to be careful not to make the mission about them. One always has the tendency to wrap personal identity in their work. He says, "When you do work that is deeply personal, it's easy to misplace validation and identity." Travis carefully protects against crossing that line and creating unhealthy habits and behaviors.

Since 2004, Global Support Mission has built a medical clinic, vocational school, preschool, and an orphanage that cares for more than sixty children. In addition, they have approximately three thousand children whom they help through subsidized health care and education. They have added another indigenous partner but continue their relationship with Faith and the work that they started in 2004.

A more recent addition within the organization is the launch of the Know. Think. Act. Initiative. Travis says, "We encountered a child with a specific need that required $600. It was a reminder that the need was much larger than what any single person or organization could meet. We had to keep thinking big."

Travis leaned on his experience and creativity to expand the effort of Global Support Mission. He says, "Technology affords us fund-raising capacity that we had to take advantage of." Rather than raising money each time for each opportunity, Travis wanted to build a micro-financing model that connected needs with people who had the capacity to fund those needs. He wanted something that someone could do wherever they were in the world and help in whatever capacity they had.

This new effort has proven to be very successful. The goal is to raise more than $1 million a year through that site, and Global Support Mission is well on their way to doing that. The new initiative has also helped more people get involved in the work, which is vitally important to spreading the message of the organization and sharing the passion to help the poor. Travis says, "Not everyone can travel around the world nor do they want to. But everyone can do something." The initiative is designed to be a catalyst for people to act on their emotions and feelings in measurable ways.

Travis maintains that the focus of Global Support Mission remains transformation. He isn't as interested in simply building a big organization or raising a lot of money. Those are certainly ways to create a bigger impact, but the purity of his intention and clarity of his vision remains intact at the core of Global Support Mission: to go after the people the world has largely ignored and show them God's love.

Discussion Questions

1. Travis lived in a lot of different places growing up that exposed him to different people in different contexts. What have you learned about other people through traveling across the country or around the world? Describe an experience that stands out in your mind.

2. Travis took the bold step of giving up a Christmas vacation to meet Faith and participate in her work in Uganda. In what ways has God called you to leave behind what is comfortable to take you to a new place? Did you go? How did it change you?

3. Travis's parents were supportive and encouraging of his interest and effort to help others. Describe a time when your family supported you as you pursued your passion. Has

there been a time when they resisted your efforts? How can you encourage someone else in your life as they seek to follow God's call on their life?

4. Global Support Mission chooses to work through local, indigenous leaders who are already doing significant work in communities instead of doing something completely independent of them. Do you agree with this decision? Why or why not? Would you have made the same decision?

5. Travis believes action moves people from sympathy to compassion. How has the decision to act on something you feel strongly about shaped you? Why is action an important step in transformation of people and cultures?

Contact Information

To learn more about this organization or to find out how you can help, please contact Global Support Mission using the information below:

Web: www.globalsupportmission.com
E-mail: info@globalsupportmission.com
Phone: 615.427.3048
Mailing Address:
305 Lutie Street
Nashville, TN 37210

Ed Nicholson

Project Healing Waters

E d Nicholson had a long and successful career in the United States military. He was one of the lucky ones, at least that's what he thought until he was diagnosed with prostate cancer in 2004. The treatment landed him in Walter Reed Army Medical Center. The good news is that his crisis has ended, but for many of the men and women returning from war, their newly mangled bodies and minds meant adjusting to a new way of life. For those soldiers, there was no going back to what they had previously known as normal.

While recovering from cancer surgery, Ed saw firsthand how war had ravaged the minds and bodies of soldiers who were willing to give their lives if necessary in service to their country. Ed decided that he could do something to aid in the health and restoration of veterans, particularly those who were disabled. Project Healing Waters utilizes fly-fishing as a way to assist in the emotional and mental healing of soldiers dealing with life after war.

Ed's Story

Ed Nicholson grew up in Wadsworth, Ohio, near Akron. He attended college at the University of North Carolina, where he became involved in the Navy ROTC (Reserve Officer's Training Corps) program. This is a college-based program for training and preparing individuals to be commissioned officers in the United States military after graduation. In exchange for a partial or full scholarship, recruits commit to a number of years of military service. The length is determined by the career and division chosen.

Ed wanted to be a high school band director and planned to only spend the necessary time in the military to fulfill his obligation, get out, and go on to live the rest of his life as a civilian. What was intended to be a few years of service turned into a career. While not part of his original plan, he wouldn't change it for anything.

"The responsibility of leading a group of men was captivating," says Ed. He started with thirty men, and his responsibility only grew over time. He moved up through the ranks and continued to be promoted throughout his entire career. Ed enjoyed moving around and seeing different places, and he always enjoyed boats, being on the water, and the outdoors.

He attended post-graduate school in Monterey, California, and then moved to New York, where he met his wife. His time in the US Navy was the perfect picture of what hard work, dedication, and commitment can return—satisfaction and fulfillment. There were never any regrets about not pursuing his interest in being a band director.

After thirty years of service, Ed retired from active duty in the military. He went to work for a local defense contractor, but in 2004 he was diagnosed with prostate cancer. He decided to have surgery, a decision that would lead him to Walter Reed Army Medical Center in Washington, D.C.

While recovering from the surgery, he noticed the soldiers around him, many of whom were very young, had life-altering medical complications that often result from war. Some had lost their ability to see or hear, while some had lost arms, legs, or both. But all of them had psychological wounds, not easily seen but very real indeed.

Ed was so touched by the need around him that he forgot about his own battle with cancer. He wanted to do something to help these disabled veterans. It was a tough task that would likely come with tremendous challenges, but he wasn't going to lie around, heal, go home, and just forget about everyone he met and everything he saw. It was all too real for him.

He loved to fly-fish and thought that he might be able to share his love for the outdoors with soldiers in desperate need for hope and healing. Perhaps fly-fishing could function as a catalyst for wholeness, unlike any drug or other medical treatment could. Ed wasn't sure if it would work but decided it was worth giving it a try.

"There is something about being in nature and in the water that just brings a sense of peace and healing," says Ed. "It's hard to focus on much else when you're in the water, so it allows your mind to slow down long enough to relax. That's when the healing begins."

The first challenge was how to get to the right person at Walter Reed to secure permission to move forward. "Walter Reed is a very large hospital with lots of different volunteer groups. Knowing which person to appeal to was a challenge," says Ed. After a few months of asking around, he connected with an occupational therapist who affirmed his idea of getting disabled veterans into nature as a part of the healing process.

The therapist recognized that physical therapy is best conducted in a controlled environment. However, occupational therapy is best conducted in real time and in real situations and scenarios. The goal of physical therapy is strength and motion while the goal of occupational therapy is to get the patient to re-enter everyday life successfully in spite of having to find a new way to do ordinary tasks like driving, cooking, personal care, etc.

Ed's argument for a fly-fishing program was solid. It was peaceful, simple, and took someone into the heart of nature. "The act of fly-fishing builds the confidence these guys need to adapt to normal life again. If I can teach a guy with one hand how to tie a fly-fishing line, I can teach him how to tie his shoes with one hand, too," he says. The occupational therapist agreed and fully supported Ed's idea.

There wasn't a lot of fanfare when Ed started taking veterans out on the water. He didn't wait until a formal organizational structure was in place. Instead, he just started doing it. The program grew from there.

Ed knew that a key ingredient to the success of Project Healing Waters early on was a genuine interest from disabled veterans. While Ed was confident his idea could help, he had no idea if anyone would sign up to participate. It was great to have the approval and oversight of the staff, but he knew without veterans, his idea was only going to remain an idea.

One of Ed's first recruits was a veteran named Robert. When they first met, Robert had lost his eye and his jaw was missing. There was a towel around Robert's neck because there was nothing he could do to keep the saliva from running out of his mouth and down his face. Robert was thirty years old when he joined the Army. He was overseas when he was involved with an explosion. After thirty to forty different operations, the doctors at Walter Reed were able to restore his face very close to its original condition. Ed and Robert immediately connected, and Robert loved the concept of Project Healing Waters. He became someone that the other injured soldiers could trust and identify with. "Robert brought a lot of credibility to what we were trying to do," Ed says. "He was a very motivational figure in the early days." Robert, with the help of the ministry, was able to heal emotionally and physically. He now works in the technology industry and has what many people would consider a normal life.

There are no requirements to participate in the program. "We've worked with blind individuals, double amputees, and even soldiers with brain injuries. We have yet to run into a scenario where we have had to deny a disabled veteran the ability to fly-fish because of a certain disability," says Ed. In fact, a veteran doesn't even have to have their own equipment; the program provides a reel and rod for them to use on outings. "Many times," says Ed, "when a veteran shows a particular affinity for fly-fishing and a commitment to the sport, they are given their own equipment."

The program quickly grew. Ed doesn't remember many objections or roadblocks that he had to scale as the program developed. "Our model was simple, and we wanted to keep it that way," he says.

Ed is aware that injured veterans increase during wartime and decrease during times of peace, but he knows that even when the war is over and all the troops are home, many will still have to deal with the physical effects of war, be that physical or mental. During times of war people tend to think more regularly about the sacrifices of the armed forces and are more likely to give to Project Healing Waters, yet Ed is not concerned about finances. Every disabled veteran that has been helped through the program has helped spread the word about the work Project Healing Waters is doing.

Most veterans are grateful for the opportunity, and their families are grateful, too. "I remember one wife who told me, 'That's my husband. You've given me my husband back. Thank you. He wasn't the same after the war.'" Ed has numerous examples of similar stories like this.

As the program caught on, a new challenge they had to figure out was a way to get the program into every Veteran's Affairs hospital across the country. There are a total of 150 hospitals, and Ed wants to have at least one chapter in every facility. The only way to accomplish this goal was to provide enough structure to duplicate the process but not be so restrictive that he inhibited growth. This was a difficult balance to strike. In fact, Ed was cautioned to grow slowly or things could get out of hand.

Ed never wanted to be in a position to have to turn someone away because they didn't have room in the program. "Our position has been from the beginning that we'll put the program out there, not do anything stupid or crazy, and run with the good ideas as they come," he says.

Early on Ed tried to franchise the idea, but that didn't work out quite like he had hoped. It was overwhelming to think about starting something new every time, having to go into a new place, establish new relationships, and teach the leaders about fly-fishing and how to run the program. That approach didn't seem effective or efficient.

He regrouped and decided to take a completely different approach. Instead of teaching potential leaders how to fly-fish and run the program, Ed went in search of people who already were fly fishermen, had a love for the outdoors, and wanted to share in the work of helping disabled veterans heal from their wounds of war. The requirements to have a chapter was fairly straightforward: a fly-fishing group that would provide volunteers and organize the fishing events, a VA hospital who would serve as the host of the program, and wounded or disabled veterans willing to participate.

Today, Project Healing Waters has more than 136 programs and is growing. This program has helped more than three thousand veterans successfully return to civilian life. However, many are returning to a civilian life that is different from the one they left behind. They have been changed in many ways by what they saw and experienced overseas.

Project Healing Waters has almost as many volunteers as they have had people go through the program. The simplicity of the program has an appeal that allows people of many different backgrounds to be a part of the program. In most places there are enough volunteers to have a one-on-one relationship between the veteran and the volunteer. This is a great way to build a personal relationship and have someone to walk through the healing process with each veteran.

As the organization developed, Ed formed a board, developed a Web site, and created the necessary organizational structure to accept tax-deductible donations. His desire to help has spurred a movement that he never could have anticipated in the early days at Walter Reed. "The feeling that you have helped somebody crosses all kinds of divides. It's unlike anything else. It can't be measured outside personal fulfillment," says Ed.

Recently Ed was asked to speak at a Memorial Day service. He encouraged the crowd to look within and find out how you can turn what you enjoy doing into a way to help other people. "We shouldn't feel like we have to volunteer to do something that we don't have a passion for. Pick something that you like to do and think about ways others can have a better life by learning the skills you already have," he says.

Project Healing Waters began with the simple desire to help others. Ed finds a great deal of satisfaction in knowing that he has found a way to couple his passion for the outdoors and fly-fishing with helping fellow veterans cope and heal from the devastating realities of war, realities that only those who endure them can ever fully understand. Ed says, "In the water these heroes forget their disability. They feel safe, and they can begin to heal."

Discussion Questions

1. Ed was unexpectedly diagnosed with prostate cancer. What unexpected things have happened in your life? How have those experiences shaped you?

2. While recovering from surgery, Ed noticed the plight of many of the soldiers in the hospital. Many times it's easy to only focus on ourselves and never recognize the needs of others around us. Describe a time when you realized that the needs of those around you were greater than the struggles you were dealing with at the time. How did this change your perspective on your situation?

3. Ed launched Project Healing Waters because he had a passion for his fellow veterans and fly-fishing. What are you passionate about that you could use as an opportunity to help others?

4. Ed never intended to start an organization. His desire was just to help a few people heal from the pain they were feeling inside. Why is it important to keep the focus on helping others rather than getting sidetracked by the details? How can the fear of complexity inhibit you from doing what you intended to do in the first place?

5. Ed believes faith is best expressed when we help others overcome their struggles. Do you agree with this? Why or why not? Give an example of how this has been true in your journey of faith.

Contact Information

To learn more about this organization or to find out how you can help, please contact Project Healing Waters using the information below:

Web: www.projecthealingwaters.org
Email: admin@projecthealingwaters.org
Mailing Address:
PO Box 695
LaPlata, MD 20646

Cle Ross

Kansas City Kids: Reviving Baseball in Inner Cities

C le Ross discovered an abandoned Little League baseball field in Kansas City, Kansas, one afternoon while out running with a friend. He was intrigued by the history of the field as some of major league baseball's most well-known players had started their journey there. After graduating from college on a baseball scholarship, Cle decided to design and build a baseball program that targeted inner-city kids.

Growing up in a single-parent home, Cle understood the financial and emotional challenges many underserved kids face due to circumstances beyond their control. He was eventually awarded an official chapter of the Reviving Baseball in Inner Cities initiative designed by major league baseball to reverse the declining number of minorities involved in the sport. Today, more than six hundred and fifty children and seventy-five adult coaches and volunteers support these children both on and off the field.

Cle's Story—

Cle Ross grew up in a single-parent household, the youngest of two boys, in Wichita, Kansas. His mom worked very hard, and they didn't have a lot, but they always had enough.

It wasn't until later when Cle realized that other people in the community understood their situation and helped them out from time to time. "Sometimes my mom didn't have enough money to buy food and pay the cable bill, but somehow our cable was never cut off," he says. One family befriended Cle and his brother, knowing how much they loved sports. From time to time, the father would drop off baseball equipment and other sporting goods for Cle and his brother to use. None of these "gifts" were ever marked. It was years later when Cle found out who was the source of these acts of generosity. He hoped he could find a way to help others in a similar fashion in the future.

Sports, whether it be wrestling, football, or baseball, has been part of Cle's life for as long as he can remember. His grandfather was the president of a Little League football program, where Cle started playing a year or two before he was technically supposed to because he showed promise. His grandfather also knew that if Cle was involved with sports, he would be less likely to get involved in gangs or drugs, or get into trouble. "Sports gave me that outlet that I needed. It was an even playing field," he says.

Faith was also a part of Cle's life from birth. His mother was the church pianist, so he was at church when he wasn't in school, on the field, or at home. Cle and his brother started singing in the church choir at the age of five, which they continued until they graduated from high school.

Cle says football came naturally to him, and he did well in wrestling. Baseball was where his older brother outperformed him, but Cle loved baseball more than any other sport. He was determined to do well. He played multiple sports throughout his high school days. But during one football game his senior year, he was injured, preventing him from playing varsity baseball.

After graduating high school, Cle walked away from a football scholarship and decided to start college and not play any sports. It was during that absence he realized just how much he loved sports, and more specifically baseball. Cle decided to take a chance and try out for the baseball team and see what would happen. While Cle would be considered a "walk-on," there were some drawbacks he would have to overcome. The key difference for a "walk-on" versus an athlete with a scholarship is the savings of tuition and book fees. Hoping not to burden his mom with the outrageous costs of books, he felt confident that he could earn a scholarship and a permanent spot on the team. His hard work paid off, and Cle did earn a baseball scholarship the following year.

Before transferring colleges, Cle and a friend were out for a run in Kansas City when they stopped to catch their breath. He looked up and noticed an abandoned Little League baseball field. It was trashed and barely looked like a field at all. It also didn't take Cle long to realize that he was in an impoverished neighborhood. In that moment Cle saw the potential that a baseball program might provide for the kids in this community. He remembered what sports had meant for him growing up, and he wanted to share that with kids who likely didn't have much hope for a better life. Cle wanted to do something, but the time was not right.

Cle went on to complete his college education, graduating with a degree in mass communications from the University of Arkansas. While his interest in broadcasting never died, the right doors never opened. Eventually he found full-time work that brought him back to Kansas City.

It wasn't long before Cle started working on his baseball league idea. He started doing some research and was astonished to find the historic nature of the ballpark that he and his friend just happened upon during that afternoon run. He learned that the field was an important part of the Negro Baseball Leagues and Little League baseball. Some of the greatest minority players to ever play in the major leagues played on this field. Nine players who played on this field went on to play professional baseball, seven of those made it to the major leagues, and four played for the Kansas City Royals.

The historical significance of this field fueled Cle's desire to restore the field in honor of those who had played and to bring sports to an area that few children would have access to. The Negro Leagues started in Kansas City and eventually merged with the major leagues. Players like Jackie Robinson and Willie Mays were able to break the racial barrier and show the world that baseball was to be enjoyed and played by everyone, not just one race.

The most difficult part of getting the program started was trying to find the person who legally owned the field. Cle spent countless hours in the library and making phone calls trying to find this person. He even hired an attorney to help. At one point the attorney encouraged Cle to stop wasting his time and move on, but he wasn't about to give up.

Finally Cle got a lead that eventually led him to the owner of the property. As long as he agreed to not allow an apartment complex to be built there, the owner would sell the property to Cle. Since the legal entity that owned the field was a nonprofit, Cle formed a nonprofit to facilitate the transaction. He says, "I promised the owner that if I didn't have the program up and running in one year, that I would give the property back."

It took an entire year to get the program in order and to get the ballpark into playable conditions. However, there was still no electricity for lights or running water for the bathroom. That was an obstacle that would have to wait. Too much damage had been done while the field sat dormant, and it would be too expensive to fix right away. Nevertheless, the kids wanted to play baseball, and that's exactly what Cle intended to let them do.

The first year 155 kids showed up for STICKS (Support Towards Inner City Kids Sports). The second year 325 kids signed up. It was during the second year of the program when Cle convinced Major League Baseball to support this program. "I told them we were targeting kids that would never play. They liked what we were doing and said yes," he says. That's when the name changed from STICKS to Kansas City Kids RBI (Reviving Baseball in Inner Cities).

The program continued to grow. In 2011 more than four hundred and fifty kids enrolled. The number grew to six hundred and fifty in 2012. It takes nearly eighty adult volunteers and coaches to operate a league. Those six hundred and fifty kids are dispersed among forty different teams and compete with each other.

For many children in the inner city, baseball was financially out of reach to them. Thus, fewer and fewer were playing at the major league level. Major League Baseball recognized this as a core reason why there was a declining number of minorities playing the game and launched an effort in 1989 to address it.

Most baseball leagues cost thousands of dollars to register. This is, of course, in addition to the cost of any travel, uniforms, and equipment. "Our kids couldn't afford it if we charged those prices," Cle says. Kansas City Kids RBI program only costs $25 to register. The program is able to secure sponsorships and private donations that cover the costs of equipment and other fees. "The registration fee we charge our kids is the same it was back in 1949," he says.

Cle has received no push back from members of the community or its leaders. "I'm shocked by all the stories I hear from random people who stop by and tell us the memories they have about the baseball field growing up. This place means a lot to them," he says. There was an active baseball league that utilized this field from 1949 to 1998. During that time the average participation was twenty-five hundred kids. Cle believes the program can grow back to that and will in a very short period of time.

Most leagues only run during the summer, where Cle runs his program year-round. "I know that if the kids are playing baseball, then they are not getting into trouble or doing drugs," he says. The weather prohibits baseball during several months of the calendar year, but during those months, Cle coordinates with various churches to use their indoor facilities to create a study hall experience.

Cle is very focused on education and encourages every child in the program to take what happens in the classroom seriously. "My mom didn't tolerate sports if my brother and I weren't doing well in class," he says. "I apply the same rules to these kids." Cle is known for sitting players out of games, even the talented ones, if their grades fall or they aren't doing well in school. "These kids don't have anyone who is pushing the value of education. Without baseball, I wouldn't have a college education. I don't want them to lose sight of that," Cle says.

Cle has given up a lot in life to run this league. In fact, just about every moment of his free time is spent on the league. He even brings his young son to the ball field to watch the other kids play. Cle wants these kids to understand that passion and commitment is what will help them accomplish things in life and make a lasting mark on the world. He tells them they are going to run into a lot of roadblocks but to keep pushing through. Cle hopes the discipline they learn from playing baseball and doing well in the classroom will one day give these kids a chance to make a better life for themselves.

"These kids remind me of myself and how I felt growing up—misunderstood," Cle says. He wants to show them love and give them a healthy example of what a father should be, something neither Cle nor many of the kids have at home. "I never want to leave anyone behind."

Discussion Questions

1. Cle had a vision for what was possible while he was still in college. He didn't turn that vision into reality until after graduation. Have you ever had an idea, dream, or vision about something, but it wasn't until later when you were able to realize that vision? Describe your experience. What can these seemingly "delayed" experiences teach us about God's timing?

2. Cle could have easily given up on his dream when it became difficult to find the owner of the field. Even his

attorney gave up on the search for the owner. Has there ever been a time in your life when you felt like you were alone in your work because everyone else had given up? How did it make you feel? What made you keep your focus and commitment to move forward?

3. Cle understood the home life of many of the kids in his program because that was once his life, too. Do you think that makes him more or less effective in his role? Why or why not? What about your life makes you uniquely suited or positioned to help others in a specific way?

4. Cle worked hard and was disciplined when it came to sports growing up. It eventually landed him a scholarship that helped him pay for college. Why is discipline just as valuable as passion? Name three people you know who had to overcome the odds in order to find a way to help others. Do you think they would say that passion is more, less, or equally important to discipline? Why?

5. Cle takes a holistic approach to his program in that he values both education and sports, even if that costs him some "wins" on the field. He wants these kids to have what they need to make a better life for themselves. List the places where you serve. Are you serving in those roles to feel good about yourself or achieve some personal goal, or are you serving in that capacity because you want to impact someone's present and future in a meaningful way?

Contact Information

To learn more about this organization or to find out how you can help, please contact Kansas City Kids: Reviving Baseball in Inner Cities using the information below:

Web: www.kckrbi.org
E-mail: registration@kckrbi.org
Phone: 913.825.6683
Mailing Address:
PO Box 12443
Kansas City, KS 66112

Haley Kilpatrick

Girl Talk

H aley Kilpatrick didn't grow up in the lap of luxury. Her parents sacrificed to send her to a nearby private school and give her every opportunity to succeed. Haley worked hard and did well in the classroom. However, she experienced teen bullying and teasing that made her want to give up many times along the way.

She was determined to prevent other girls from experiencing the same things she had experienced during middle school. What she started in high school as an attempt to draw attention to the issue and provide a simple solution for bullying has exploded into an organization known as Girl Talk. With $10,000 of her own money, the support of those who believed in her, and a burning desire to continue to help girls feel empowered instead of bullied, Girl Talk now reaches more than thirty-four thousand girls in forty-three states and four countries around the world.

Haley's Story

Haley Kilpatrick is the oldest of three siblings. She grew up in Albany, Georgia, a blue-collar community where most people are born, raised, live, and die. The Kilpatricks are fifth-generation residents of Albany. Her parents worked hard for what they had but never went to college. It wasn't because they weren't smart enough. Rather, they were never encouraged to do so. This would change for Haley and her siblings.

Haley remembers having a very happy childhood. She never had an abundance, but she always had enough. Haley, like most children, was not aware of what she didn't have until she was put into an environment where she realized that she had a lot more than some and a lot less than others.

The power of generosity was something Haley experienced very early in life. Her mom had a rare eye disease and the surgery she needed was not covered by insurance. There was no way her parents could afford to pay for the procedure so the family prayed intently about it. One Christmas morning a check appeared that was enough to cover the cost of the surgery. "I learned that Christ is most clear when Christianity is practiced outside the walls of the church and in the community," she says.

Haley's parents chose to send her to an inner-city elementary magnet school. "My parents wanted us to have a very clear picture of the real world and the needs of other people," she says. That meant she had to be bussed into an impoverish part of town. "I went to school with kids who didn't have clean clothes to wear," says Haley. One particular student named Robert still stands out in her mind. The teacher put his name on the board because he didn't have a pencil and paper to use in class. Haley didn't understand why he did not bring a pencil and paper to class, so she finally found the courage to ask him why he didn't have his school supplies. He told her that his parents couldn't afford to buy the supplies he needed.

Haley went home and told her mom about what had happened and what Robert said. Her mom encouraged her to figure out a solution to help Robert. "I was scared and overwhelmed at the same time," she says. "I wanted to help, but I didn't know how." She decided to sell popcorn and lemonade from a homemade stand. Haley's younger brother and sister also helped her. She raised a couple hundred dollars and was able to buy enough school supplies that Robert would never have to get in trouble again. "I still look back at this experience as one that was key in shaping who I am today," says Haley.

Haley's mom taught her to respect everyone no matter what kind of clothes they wore, title they had, or how much money they made. One day Haley and her mother walked past the school janitor, but Haley only spoke to the school principal. Her mom made sure that Haley knew how disappointed she was that Haley didn't speak to the janitor. From that day forward Haley always looks at others as equals, even if society says that they aren't.

When it was time for middle school, Haley's parents decided that it was best for her to attend a private school to help prepare her for college, something her parents felt was non-negotiable for their daughter. "My parents gave up a lot to send me to this particular school. I didn't want to let them down," says Haley.

Haley's mom took her shopping for school, and she was so excited about her new school clothes. On the first day of school, Haley discovered that there were brands of clothes that she had never heard of but was convinced were much more expensive than what she had on. She remembers feeling out of place from day one, and the constant stares didn't help. This was the beginning of three years of ups and downs. "There were a few good days and then a few bad days," says Haley. She was devastated because she never received an invitation to things like weekend sleepovers, especially from the girls she regularly had lunch with.

Feeling out of place at school became normal. The stares continued, the invitations never came, and the slurs hurt each and every time they were spoken. One particular nickname Haley remembers was "Crisco." This was given to her because she was the greasy girl from the other side of town.

The most daunting place was the cafeteria. She remembers trying to sit next to one girl, but the girl put her purse down as a way to tell Haley that she could not sit there. Sometimes the criticism from her peers came as a result of unexpected things like the type of sandwich bags her mom used to pack her lunch. The girls at school thought she should use the bags that clasp together. Haley's mom purchased the ones that simply folded over. "My mom bought those because more came to a pack than the ones that clasped together," says Haley. "I understood her reasoning, but I didn't like her decision."

When Haley finally had enough bullying, she demanded that her mom take her to Target. She was going to use some of her own money, what little she had saved, and purchase a box of the sandwich bags that clasped together. Her mom didn't understand what made the type of sandwich bags she used so important, but mostly she didn't like that Haley was becoming obsessed with things that really didn't matter.

Instead of trying to find the perfect sandwich bag, her mom connected her to the local literacy center. Haley's mom wanted her to spend time with someone she could help teach to read instead of focusing on her own self and problems. While there, Haley met a fourteen-year-old mother who didn't know how to read. This young mother had come to the literacy center because her young son would soon be old enough to read, and she was embarrassed that she would not be able to teach him. This began a two-year relationship where Haley would teach this young mother how to read and write with the help of a few teachers she had befriended at school.

Haley's school experience began to change when she tried out for the dance team. She was paired with an older high school student who would mentor her. The older girl explained that Haley's middle school troubles would soon disappear once she entered high school. She was relieved until she realized her youngest sister was about to enter middle school. Haley feared that she would have a similar experience.

Haley's mentor experience with the older high school student gave her the idea of creating a safe place where girls could talk about their struggles, be affirmed, and build strong relationships, self-confidence, and self-esteem in the process. After speaking with a few of her teachers, Haley discussed her idea with her mother, who said, "If you're concerned about your sister and other girls going through what you experienced, then do something about it." That was all Haley needed to move forward.

The headmaster gave Haley his blessing to develop a peer-to-peer mentoring program to address school bullying. She mailed a letter to all the parents as the summer was coming to a close and the new school year was about to begin. Haley had no idea how many girls would show up at the first meeting. She was very nervous. Speaking in front of other people was not something that came natural to her. "I wanted to change the hallways of our school. Middle school students are influenced by older students even more than their parents in many ways," she says.

A classroom had been chosen as the meeting place. When eighty girls showed up for the first meeting, they had to move to the library. Haley says, "If God wasn't involved in the initial stages, none of this would have happened."

One metaphor Haley uses to describe how important Girl Talk can be in the lives of young girls is a wrapped gift. She says, "We don't leave wrapped gifts under the Christmas tree. Instead, we quickly rip off the wrapping paper, no matter how beautiful or expensive, to see what's inside." Haley believes that's how girls should treat one another. "We should disregard what's on the outside and work intently on seeing the gift within every girl."

By the time Haley graduated from high school, there were eight different Girl Talk programs in the local area. She had no idea what to do with this idea when she first attended college. Like many, Haley wanted to have a normal college experience, moving to Atlanta as a first step toward discovering a bigger world than what she knew growing up.

Yet Haley couldn't escape Girl Talk. After a small feature in *Cosmo Girl* in 2004, the editor sent her a box of 737 letters. The editor included a note that encouraged Haley not to stop what she was doing with Girl Talk because it was resonating with people. She explained that the response the magazine received from the article was more than they typically receive for a single feature. This confirmed for Haley that Girl Talk was what she wanted to do full-time.

Expanding Girl Talk would not be easy. It didn't take long for Haley to realize that there was little funding available for start-up nonprofit organizations. "Most people expect you to fail. At least that's how you feel," she says. Haley had saved a little money but did not have access to unlimited resources. Peer-to-peer fundraising seemed to be the most effective method to build a program around. When she asked, people responded generously. "When you get in front of the right person, you find that people have big hearts," she says.

One example is when Haley approached a newly founded design firm. The founder agreed to help Haley build the Web site for no money because he had a daughter and wanted to help. That working relationship continues today. "The amazing thing is we were able to reach the first fifteen thousand girls with less than $10,000 cash. Girl Talk was able to secure a lot of gifts-in-kind to cover the gaps," she says.

There have been a lot of people along the way who have tried to discourage Haley and her work with Girl Talk. She says, "When God calls you to do something, you have the innate ability to turn down the noise." Haley doesn't internalize the negative things people say to her. She believes some people have a limited perspective. She says, "Some people are like chickens who can only see the ground. Other people are like song birds who have a much bigger perspective because they can fly. So listen to the song birds and ignore the chickens."

Haley has continued to push Girl Talk to reinvent itself and expand its offerings. A recent expansion in the organization was to begin a summer camp. Some board members didn't want to expand into this space because the model was very different from what Girl Talk had ever done. It became a wild success where girls of means and girls with little means mix, learn from each other, and find value in each other as individuals, instead of the brands they wear or the things their parents own.

Haley says, "If you want to make an impact but don't know where to get started, look for your valley moment. Find what frustrates you and look for your opportunity there." She believes you can't find your mountaintop until you understand the depths of the valley. Offering the same advice her mom gave her, she says, "Everyone has a desire to be significant and have a purpose. What are you going to do about it?"

Discussion Questions

1. Haley was born into a working-class family that believed education was important. Her parents worked hard and sacrificed to be able to send Haley to a local private school. How have other people helped you get where you are today? Who have you helped in a similar way?

2. Haley recognized early on that not everybody has access to things like food, clean clothes, and a stable home environment. While you may not feel like you have much, it is likely that you have more than many people you know. Describe the first time you recognized that you had more than someone else. What experience brought about that revelation? How did it make you feel? Does it make you more or less willing to help other people? Why or why not?

3. Haley's parents taught her to think about solutions to problems rather than simply focus on the problems. Which is

easier: focusing on problems or solutions? Why is it important to take action when we recognize a need rather than simply make an observation and move on? When have you tried to address a problem you noticed? What happened?

4. Haley was in high school when she started Girl Talk. She didn't allow her age, inexperience, or lack of funding to keep her from moving forward. What has God called you to do today that you are avoiding because of age, experience, or finances? In what ways do you feel unqualified to help others? How can you overcome those feelings and follow through on the work God has called you, and gifted you, to accomplish?

5. Haley took a very difficult experience and turned it into an opportunity to help others. How does God transform our wounds into the strength and resolve we need to show love toward others? Identify a time in your life when this happened. Share your experience and what you learned with at least one other person.

Contact Information

To learn more about this organization or to find out how you can help, please contact Girl Talk using the information below:

Web: www.desiretoinspire.org
E-mail: www.desiretoinspire.org/contactus.aspx

Phone: 404.442.5605
Mailing Address:
3490 Piedmont Road NE
Suite 1104
Atlanta, GA 30305

Jordan Thomas

Jordan Thomas Foundation

J ordan Thomas was the perfect picture of the American teenager. He was the only son of two successful doctors, he enjoyed sports and the outdoors, was successful both in and out of the classroom, and very popular. But at the age of sixteen the life Jordan knew changed instantly after a tragic boating accident off the coast of the Florida Keys. With the loss of both of his legs, Jordan now depends on prosthetics to walk.

After the accident Jordan quickly realized that access to quality health care and necessary prosthetics was not something every child was guaranteed. He founded the Jordan Thomas Foundation to raise money to purchase prosthetics for children and teenagers who desperately needed them but could not afford the out-of-pocket expenses. In addition,

Jordan has expanded his efforts into public policy in an attempt to create greater awareness around the needs of the people who depend on prosthetics and to reform industry and insurance practices related to replacement limbs.

Jordan's Story

Jordan Thomas was a healthy sixteen-year-old boy and enjoyed life in all its fullness. He played sports, did well in the classroom, and was popular among his peers. His future was bright.

Jordan's parents, both successful doctors, enjoyed watching their only child grow up before their eyes. They had many family trips, several involving water sports. A trip to the Florida Keys was shaping up to be just another wonderful experience when a tragic accident happened to Jordan. He and his family were about five miles off the coast when Jordan jumped in the water to scuba dive with his dad. The waves were particularly high and rippled across the water. Somehow Jordan got pushed outside the view of his mom and dad. Fearing that Jordan might end up under the boat or pulled away by the current, his mom quickly started the engine to move the boat forward. Only Jordan was behind the boat, instead of away or under it.

When his mom started up the boat, the engine sucked Jordan into it and cut off his two legs from the knees down. He didn't realize what had happened at first. "It was the most surreal feeling because I didn't feel any pain. But I was very present and knew what was going on."

Jordan was airlifted to a local hospital where the doctors were able to stabilize his body. He spent the next thirteen consecutive days in recovery before he was released to go home and into rehabilitation. While there, he started interacting with the other kids.

Jordan never doubted he would be able to obtain the prosthetics he needed to help him walk again, but it hadn't occurred to him that this was not the case for every child he met who needed them. It didn't take long for him to realize that many of the kids he was talking to and playing with didn't have parents who were financially able to cover any and all costs related to prosthetic limbs. It was a difficult reality to come to grips with, and it didn't make sense to Jordan.

He says, "I remember wondering who was going to help them get what they needed if their parents weren't able to do it." It was during this time when Jordan got the idea to help the other children get the prosthetics they needed. It was the beginning of a journey for Jordan, learning to live with prosthetics but also figuring out how he was going to help others get them too.

"It was during the accident when God became real to me," says Jordan. Faith had been a part of his life, but he hadn't really taken it seriously. "I can't explain the peace I felt at the moment of the accident other than God's presence," he says. "The hands of God were holding me in the moment of the accident. From that point forward I have never doubted God." Jordan had some time to process his emotions while he was in the hospital. He says, "Faith was a big part of my recovery." Jordan never felt bad about himself. While he admits that he recognized his life would never be the same, he felt a strong sense to help the other kids in the hospital. Jordan says, "I felt like I had been given so much that it was now my turn to give back."

His parents told him that life would bring various challenges, but how he responded would determine whether or not he would overcome the challenge or be overcome by it. They told him to name the problem he was facing and figure out a solution. That would ensure success every time. This type of thinking was deeply embedded in Jordan's mind and certainly played a role in how things developed both during and after recovery.

The life of a double amputee is very different from someone who still has their legs. "You always have a wheelchair close by," says Jordan. "I take my legs off at the end of a long day like most people take off their shoes." The most challenging part of life is not necessarily physical but psychological and emotional. It often takes a long time to make peace with a new, modified way of living.

It would take Jordan about two years to get over the public stares and get comfortable with a new routine and pace of living. "My doctors told me that I'd likely never play golf again. I'm proud to say that I play golf regularly today with a plus one handicap. That's better than scratch," he says. Jordan has been able to exceed every goal and expectation he and his family, as well as his doctors, had for his recovery.

Jordan's parents knew what it meant to be generous in many different ways. Whether it was a community event or church fund-raiser, his parents always contributed something or volunteered in some way. One experience stands out in his mind. One time his mom observed a mother and child walking home with groceries in hand. Jordan remembered his mom pulled over, asked them to get in, drove them home, and then gave them an envelope with $500. "I never knew how much was in there until later. I have never forgotten that experience. This is the type of generosity I saw from my parents on a regular basis," says Jordan.

Jordan was raised to never look down on anyone, no matter their skin color, financial status, or job title. Everyone was equal and had a responsibility to care for one another. He says, "My parents told me that I was fortunate to have all that I did. That meant that I had a responsibility to make sure everyone was given a fair chance." In spite of having so much, Jordan was able to keep a very grounded perspective about life.

He admitted that he knew very little about prosthetics before his accident. Jordan's legs cost $13,000. The top-end prosthetics can cost as much as $100,000 or more per prosthetic limb. That amount of money will bankrupt most families.

"Most providers," Jordan says, "only cover a portion of the cost or only cover one fitting." This frustrated him because he knew that many kids couldn't cover the cost of one set of prosthetics, let alone replacements necessary due to use and growth. "Giving a child one set of prosthetics is like giving them one pair of shoes and telling them to wear that same pair for the rest of their lives. It's ridiculous," says Jordan.

Jordan didn't waste any time acting on his commitment to help other children get the prosthetics they needed. The first prosthetic recipient was a little girl from a Mennonite family. She needed one above-the-knee prosthetic and one below-the-knee prosthetic. The joy of watching this little girl walk again was unbelievable. This took place nine months after Jordan's accident. He knew that to be able to help others would involve raising awareness and money. "Only about two million people live with a limb loss of some kind. And only 4 percent are children. This is a very small, niche part of the population," he says. Once you know someone living with this reality, it becomes easy to recognize the need.

Jordan knew that in order to be able to expand his work and help many children, he would have to raise a lot more money in a more systematic way than just personally asking for private donations or depending on sporadic speaking engagements to stir the hearts of potential donors. He had no particular experience in raising money or hosting fundraising events, but he was convinced that this was the logical next step.

The first formal fund-raising event was held about two years after his accident. Jordan didn't realize how many moving parts were involved in pulling off something like this. He didn't know what to expect to raise either. "The one thing I remember about that first event is the overwhelming kindness and generosity I experienced. People truly wanted to help other people; they just needed an outlet and something to believe in," says Jordan.

The first fund raising goal was $500,000. The foundation raised that within three years. Everyone involved, including Jordan, was thrilled with the results. Every year Jordan and his team learned more about what worked and what didn't. This is part of what has made the Jordan Thomas Foundation so successful.

The biggest obstacle Jordan has had to face is the industry itself. "This is an incredibly profitable industry that very few people are paying much attention to," says Jordan. "If we're going to see things change, we have to put pressure on the manufacturers and providers to bring costs down. This is the only way to ensure every child has the prosthetics they need to live as normal of a life as possible." He isn't accepting business as usual even if change is a long shot. Jordan has come too far to not believe the impossible is possible.

To help spur change within the industry and insurance companies, Jordan has expanded his efforts to include influencing public policy. "I want to attack the issue on all fronts," he says. "We have to go after the insurance providers to expand their coverage, the industry providers to lower costs, and the legislature to make sure we are able to keep things moving forward." Jordan believes this population, while small, deserves to be represented and cared for.

He has been invited to Capitol Hill on several occasions to address lawmakers in person. "The conversation of health-care reform is ripe in our country. I want to make sure the needs of the prosthetic-dependent community are represented accurately and completely to the people who can help do something about it," says Jordan.

One notable difference in Jordan's approach is that his focus is on eliminating the need for the Jordan Thomas Foundation to exist. "I hope that one day there will be no need for what we do because access to prosthetics will never be an issue for anyone," Jordan says. Where many nonprofits and foundations want to make a difference, the Jordan Thomas Foundation hopes to put itself out of business one day in the not-so-distant future. He says, "Hopefully, I will be unemployed because no one needs what we do anymore."

Jordan believes that he and the efforts of the Jordan Thomas Foundation have just scratched the surface of what's possible. As the foundation has grown, Jordan has assembled a small staff to continue to expand the infrastructure to support the change he wants to see take place. He believes having the right systems in place will ensure ultimate success.

He plans to continue to press forward even while he studies Spanish and International Business in college. Jordan believes he is just like anyone else who wants to make a difference. He doesn't believe that he has something others don't have. Jordan has simply made the commitment to use his life as an instrument of change. He says, "I want to fight for and give a voice to people who have traditionally not been given a voice."

Jordan thinks having a heart of gratitude for who you are and what you have, even if you are disabled, is what has to exist in the hearts and lives of people who want to make a difference. He has learned three keys to taking on the task of helping others. They are to never fear asking for help, surrounding yourself with good people who know more than you do, and never lose focus of what you want to accomplish. Jordan says, "My accident was the biggest blessing and miracle. I know that at my core."

Discussion Questions

1. Jordan took a tragic situation and used it as an opportunity to make a difference. How have you turned a difficult situation or setback into an opportunity to help others? Describe what happened, what you did, and how it changed you.

2. Jordan started the Jordan Thomas Foundation while he was still a teenager because he felt a sense of urgency around the need. Think about a time when you felt unqualified to serve but knew the opportunity was right to act. What happened? How did you respond? What did you learn about yourself? About God?

3. Jordan never had to worry about being able to pay the high costs of prosthetics, yet he recognized that not every child was as fortunate as he was. Identify three things you are

grateful for in your life. How does our level of gratitude affect our willingness to help others? Explain.

4. Jordan recognized that little attention was being given to prosthetics and the people who use them by insurance companies, hospitals, and prosthetic manufacturers, so he decided to raise awareness, especially around the need for public policy reform. How have you been uniquely positioned to be an advocate for someone else?

5. Jordan believes strongly in finding a permanent solution to funding prosthetics for every child and teenager in need. He hopes one day there will no longer be a need for an organization like the Jordan Thomas Foundation because the right prosthetics will be available to those who need them. In what ways does the search for a permanent solution change our approach to creating change? What level of commitment do you think it takes to provide a permanent solution rather than a temporary one? Are you willing to strive to bring about permanent solutions for the people you are most passionate about serving?

Contact Information

To learn more about this organization or to find out how you can help, please contact Jordan Thomas Foundation using the information on the next page:

Web: www.jordanthomasfoundation.org
E-mail: info@jordanthomasfoundation.org
Phone: 423.622.9006
Mailing Address:
PO Box 22764
Chattanooga, TN 37422

Thom and Michele Hazelip

Front Porch Ministry

T hom and Michele Hazelip, along with their four children, lived comfortably in the suburbs until God disrupted their world and called them to do something extraordinary. A real estate investment opportunity turned into a divine invitation to give up a comfortable life in the suburbs to move into a part of the inner-city of Nashville, marked by prostitution, criminal activity, and poverty. After much prayer and consideration, they decided to make the move, a decision that few of their friends and family could comprehend at the time.

Front Porch Ministry is an accurate description of Thom and Michele's approach to sharing God's love with others. They believe that relationships and authentic community are the only way to make a true impact and see transformation take place. By involving themselves in the everyday lives of people often written off and dismissed by many, Thom and Michele have become active members of this troubled community and daily meet the physical, spiritual, and practical needs of their neighbors. The result of their work is nothing less than a miracle.

Thom and Michele's Story

Thom and Michele Hazelip were living examples of the American Dream. Their families had worked hard to give them both everything they needed in life to be successful. They both completed college, found great jobs, and were moving up in the world. But no one, including Thom and Michele, expected their lives to unfold quite like it has.

Michele grew up in California, within a family of law enforcement. She studied public relations and marketing in college, and later landed a great job in the hospitality industry. After becoming a Christian at age twenty-five, she started searching for something more fulfilling than the next big promotion and the next big raise.

Thom grew up in Alabama, a son of a pastor. By the time he was in ninth grade, Thom was already managing more than one hundred speaking engagements a year for his father, who was in a very conservative denomination. Thom loved sports and would, for a short period of time, work as a college basketball coach and bi-vocational pastor. He later shifted careers and became a successful technology consultant.

Michele's immediate family was not religious. The first person she called after becoming a believer was her aunt who lived in Memphis, Tennessee. Her aunt eventually played matchmaker, introducing Thom and Michele on the phone. After an initial awkward silence, they started talking, and the conversations continued over the next several months. Thom decided to fly out to meet Michele in person and, as they say, the rest is history. Nine months later they were married.

In spite of all their unique differences, there was one area where they were absolutely identical—they both strongly believed and practiced hospitality. Thom's consulting business was extremely successful. He became interested in real estate as an investment opportunity, so like many, he started flipping houses as a way to turn a hobby into some extra money.

Thom and Michele lived in an exclusive suburban neighborhood. They were doing all the things that Americans were supposed to do—start a business, make a lot of money, live in a nice home, buy nice things, and raise a perfect family. Life was good, and they were enjoying themselves and their "perfect" life.

While driving around town one day after a consulting meeting, Thom stumbled onto a house in a not-so-great part of town. It was a beautiful, spacious home on a corner lot. But like many homes in the area, it had not been kept up and needed some work. Thom thought it was a great investment. He thought he could purchase the home for a fraction of what the owner was asking, spend a little money fixing it up, and then sell it for a nice profit.

"I thought I had stumbled onto a great investment property. But then I started having a crazy dream about living in that house," says Thom. He couldn't shake the feeling that there was something more to this house than just an investment opportunity, but he didn't know why. Thom decided to purchase the property, but he and Michele wrestled with what to do with the house for months. "We didn't know if we should flip it or fix it up for us to live in," says Michele. It was a time of great prayer and conversation in Thom and Michele's marriage. To give up their "perfect life," especially with a young family, would change everything. They knew the implications of their decision. "Sometimes God calls you to live disproportionate to who you are," says Thom.

The decision to move into a crime-ridden neighborhood and on a corner known for prostitution and drugs meant living a very different life than the one they had worked so hard to build. Eventually Thom and Michele decided to make the move. "Neither our friends nor our family understood our decision," says Michele. "Everyone thought we were absolutely crazy. And to be honest, we knew what we were doing was a little crazy." But they also knew that they wanted to do more than just send money to someone else to solve what they were seeing happening in this community. They wanted to get involved in the lives of these people.

Making the decision to move turned out to be the easiest part of the process. It took eighteen months to prepare the house for them to live in it. "Things didn't get easier after our decision to move; in fact, they got tougher," says Michele. At the same time, they put their suburban home on the market and experienced little interest from buyers. The circumstances brewing created a perfect storm, and everyone seemed to be mounting their ammunition in hopes that Thom and Michele would reconsider their decision. Their beautiful home eventually sold, and Michele, Thom, and their two daughters and young son moved into their new home. What Thom had dreamed about for almost two years had become reality.

"Those first months were tough," says Thom. "Our neighbors didn't trust us, and many didn't like the idea that a white family was moving into their neighborhood." To be fair, the only white people many of these people knew were cops, and their general interactions with them were not pleasant.

One week after moving in, Michele found out she was pregnant with their fourth child. It was all overwhelming and certainly a moment of self-doubt. "We both looked at each other and wondered if we had heard God clearly," says Michele. Still, they never doubted their decision and trusted God knew what He was doing.

Thom remembers spending time meeting his neighbors with a local pastor one afternoon. The guy who lived behind their house was not at all pleased with their decision to move into his neighborhood. In fact, he refused to shake Thom's hand. "It was the first time that I had seen rage like that on someone's face. He was a big guy, and I'm convinced that had

I not been with someone he respected, I might have felt that rage in some physical way."

It took a long time to work through the skepticism of their neighbors and start to build trust with them. The primary way they were able to do that was through the children in the neighborhood who didn't seem as reluctant to trust the Hazelips as the adults. "I was shocked at how eager the kids were to come to our home. They came with open hearts and a pure desire to be loved on," says Michele.

Michele believes that while it was scary to think about bringing another child into the world given the new circumstances of their life, she believes it was a catalyst for breaking through to the people they wanted to reach. "There is something disarming about puppies and pregnant people," says Michele. "Watching me waddle around the house and down the street was something that every other mother we encountered could relate to." Michele felt like others would see someone they could relate to because they had been pregnant once, too.

One thing that Thom and Michele learned early on was that this community cared for each other. They suffered together, they shared what they had, and they were available for one another. "That isn't something you always get in the suburbs," says Thom. "Most of the time it's a casual wave and a friendly hi, but you never really get involved in the lives of the people around you," says Michele.

Soon, about thirty kids from the neighborhood could be found playing in the front yard and sitting on the porch of the

Hazelips' home on any given day. Their home had become a metaphor for community, and it all began on their front porch. So when Thom and Michele decided to make this their life's work and give up their jobs, they called it Front Porch Ministry.

"When people ask what we do, I tell them that we live in a soup kitchen," says Thom. They are actively involved in helping the families who live around them deal with the stuff of life, much of which is difficult to get your hands around. Some of it, though, is just a matter of feeling overwhelmed and needing to share the burden with someone else.

Michele remembers a time when a mother became worried about her daughter after she wasn't at her bus stop one afternoon. The mother came over to the Hazelips' and asked for help. Michele immediately got in the car with her and drove around the neighborhood. The little girl was safe but just wasn't where she was supposed to be. "The lives of the people around us aren't all that different from ours. You can choose to spend all your energy focused on the crime. If you do, you'll miss the people and the beauty of this community," she says.

Through Front Porch Ministry, Thom and Michele are able to help these families care for their children, get through tough times, find jobs, get access to food when money is tight, deal with domestic violence, go to court to show support, and a variety of other things that most people would simply consider being a good neighbor. "We believe in these kids and their families, and we want them to know that," says

Michele. Life can be hard if you have to do everything on your own and the deck is already stacked against you.

In addition to the essential things, Thom and Michele try to provide things that many people take for granted. When they realized that many of the families didn't have a family portrait, they coordinated with a local photographer to take pictures of each of the families. "Kids love to see their pictures on the wall. It's one way they learn that someone loves them and they have a place where they belong," says Michele.

Thom and Michele both admit that their decision still comes with some shocking realities. Their children are sometimes scared at night when they hear gunshots. Like many kids, they have expressed a desire to move and have a "normal" life. And there have even been times when they've been afraid to leave the house.

"It is overwhelming and stressful at times," says Michele. "But our resolve has never been shaken. And, ultimately, our children know that we love them. We do have boundaries, and we work hard to make sure we spend exclusive time with our children," says Thom and Michele.

Thom says, "What we've learned about ourselves through this process is that we had the wrong value system. We were Christians, but we didn't allow it to inform others by how we lived our lives. For example, I used to feel the need to be thanked and acknowledged when I performed an act of charity. Now I don't need that because I'm simply responding to the grace that God has shown me," says Thom. "Our value of a car is not what brand or how new it is. The value of a car in our minds is how many kids we can get in it," says Michele.

Front Porch Ministry is filling the gap between what public schools, social services, and single parents can do for children. "It's hard to do well in school if you are going to school on an empty stomach because there is no food in your house," says Thom. They host a variety of social gatherings at their home, which is where they discover many of the needs of the families in this community. Whether it's movie and popcorn night or a summer ice cream social, Thom and Michele provide a safe place for these children and their families to discover that someone does care about them, someone will walk alongside them, and most important, no matter what, they don't have to face life feeling alone.

And their hard work and relational investments have paid off. Several of the children they started working with after they first moved into the community have graduated high school and gone onto college. "These are first-generation college students. We are so proud of them," says Michele.

"Sometimes it only takes one sentence, one act of kindness to make a huge impact on someone. Ministry happens when we are in relationship with other people. One act of love can make a difference," says Thom.

Discussion Questions

1. Thom and Michele lived the life that many people aspire to have. When you were growing up or in your early

twenties, what did you think your perfect life would look like? How has that changed over time?

2. Thom and Michele decided to move from the suburbs to an inner-city neighborhood. If God had called you and your family to make a similar move, would you be willing to go? Is there a limit to your willingness to be faithful to God's call? Be honest.

3. The Gospels spend a lot of time capturing encounters Jesus had with real people. Thom and Michele believe spiritual transformation only takes place within relationships and authentic community. Why do you think Jesus spent so much time with people? Who are you building genuine relationships with? Are they just like you? If not, how are they different?

4. Thom and Michele have opened their home to their neighbors. How can the practice of hospitality show God's love to others?

5. Front Porch Ministry is an example of how one family can make a difference in a difficult place. What difference can you make right where you are? Is God calling you to leave something behind and follow Him into a difficult place? Are you willing to go?

Contact Information

To learn more about this organization or to find out how you can help, please contact Front Porch Ministry using the information below:

Web: www.frontporchministry.org
E-mail: frontporchministry@gmail.com
Mailing Address:
PO Box 281827
Nashville, TN 37228

Conclusion

Put Unconditional Love into Action

E ach of the individuals and organizations written about in this book grew up in different locations, exist within different socioeconomic realities, and possess different levels of education and experience. None of them felt prepared or qualified for the paths they felt compelled to take. All of them, however, were, and continue to be, unwavering in their decision to disrupt their normal lives and begin looking for ways to reach out and show unconditional love to others.

We create a lasting legacy by choosing to invest ourselves in others. In order to do that, we must grow past thinking that we are at the center of our own universe. Our world becomes very small when everything is about the pursuit of our personal pleasure. It's impossible for unconditional love to exist when everything is about us. We only make room for unconditional love when we recognize the recipient doesn't have the capacity to return it.

Affluence has made it difficult for many of us to comprehend a world of limitations. We find it frustrating when we have to wait to eat at our favorite restaurant while a mother might not eat that day so that her child can have what he or she needs to survive. We gladly stand in line for hours to be the first one to purchase the latest electronic device while another family gets up in the middle of the night to get in line at the local free clinic to be certain they will be seen by a doctor that day. We quickly avoid someone who doesn't look or talk like us while a woman recently released from prison feels overwhelmed at the idea of finding clean clothes to change into, a safe place to live, and a way to make a life without a healthy family system to support her.

If you've taken the time to read the stories in this book, it's likely because you want to make a difference, too. You recognize that life is more than just accumulating material things, striving for success, and achieving the peak of our profession. There has to be more to life because none of the things that are supposed to make us feel complete ever do.

The people you just read about were ordinary people who chose to leverage what they had to meet a need that was in front of them. The purity of their passion can be traced back to their sense of purpose and meaning. What we have been given in intellect, money, and opportunity is not simply ours to possess but assets to be invested in the people around us.

God did not intend for us to live lives disconnected from the people around us. Rather, He wants us to invest in people through relationships and authentic community. It is when we recognize that we are all children of God in need of a Savior that we find the strength to reach across economic, political, and social boundaries and touch the life of another person.

Jesus was clear in His purpose in coming to earth: "For the Son of Man has come to seek and to save the lost" (Luke 19:10). As followers of Jesus, we must ensure that what we seek after is consistent with the character and motives of the One we profess to follow. When our lives are consistent with the calling and ministry of Christ, we become instruments of change in the hands of Almighty God. We must no longer turn our heads to the lost, hurting, and broken. That's not what Jesus would do. And that's not what we are called to do either.

Perhaps you're thinking what could *you* possibly do to help someone else. With so much pain and so many people in need, how can *you* make a difference? Begin right where you are.

None of the people featured in this book set out to start a formal organization, be recognized nationally, or raise a lot of money. Instead, they started exactly where you are right now, with a desire for significance and a hope that they, too, could make a difference in the life of someone in need. What happened as a result of their courage and obedience was nothing short of a miracle.

There is transformational power in the midst of unconditional love. It is available to everyone who has been touched by the grace of God to freely give and receive. We must believe and act on that which we know is true. The evidence of our faith is revealed when we put our faith into action.

The difference between the individuals featured in this book and you are less than what you might think. They made a choice to act on the opportunities they saw to reach a particular group of people who needed to see and experience unconditional love. You can make a similar decision, too.

You may never start a nonprofit organization. You may never be featured in the national news. You may never be recognized beyond a small group of people, or even just one. But to those whom you show unconditional love, you will never be forgotten.

If you've ever walked through an old graveyard, you might notice that over time the wind, sun, and rain can erode the names and dates etched in stone. Once that marker has been completely wiped clean, no one will be able to read what was written. What we thought was so important won't really matter. The only thing that will count will be the mark we made on the life of another.

No one will remember how much money you made, what kind of car you drove, or the number of square feet that made up your home. The truth is no one cares about those things as much as we think they do. What people will remember are the few individuals who took the time to show them unconditional love.

You have the ability to change the world. It starts with taking what you say you believe and finding measurable ways to put your faith into action. What we think isn't real until we say it out loud. In turn, what we say can't be measured until we act upon it.

Make no mistake about it, change doesn't take place without action. And unconditional love cannot be shared without someone giving it away without regard or expectation for anything in return. The very idea of unconditional love is revolutionary. Unconditional love was God's plan for redemption from the beginning.

In the final section of this book, you'll find some tools to assist you as you contemplate the ways you can put unconditional love into action right where you are. These tools will help guide your thinking and what you are doing. Consider inviting a few other people to take this journey with you.

Remember, whatever you choose to do doesn't have to be done with great fanfare, creativity, or even a lot of money. The substance of your intentions will be measured by your willingness to share the unconditional love of God with others. Someone in your life needs to know they are loved, cared for, and has an advocate to speak on their behalf. Who is that person in your life?

Money can buy a lot of things. Power can defeat ominous opponents. Positions can exert great influence. But love, unconditional love, can't be contained, deterred, blocked, or inhibited. Instead, it is multiplied when we release it into the life of someone else.

What is your decision? Will you choose to live a normal life? Or will you find the courage to break free of the mundane and do something radical? Will you share the unconditional love of God with someone else, the same kind of love that has been freely shared with you through Jesus on the cross?

Unconditional love changes everything, yet its power can only be accessed when we give it away. Who will you love unconditionally today?

Make Your Life Count

A Guided Journaling Exercise

D o you ever ride by a cemetery and think about all the lives that are represented by the memorials? For many people, the memorial sums up their existence. Other people, however, make a more lasting impression on the world around them.

God has entrusted life to you. He has given you time, talents, resources, influence, intelligence, personality, and passion that are intended to be used for His glory. It's easy to take ownership of some of the things God entrusts to you. When that happens, life gets out of balance.

How do you keep your life focused on God?

_____

_____

Of all that God has entrusted to you, what are you most tempted to take ownership of?

_____

_____

God wants your life to matter. Just before the Israelites were taken into Babylonian exile, God said, "For I know the plans I have for you"—this is the LORD's declaration—"plans for your welfare, not for disaster, to give you a future and a hope" (Jer. 29:11).

Look at that verse closely. God has a good plan for your life. You don't have to come up with your own plan; simply trust Him and His plan. This is significant because knowing God's plan is as simple as knowing God. The closer you are to Him, the more certain you'll be of His plan for your life.

You probably are aware of situations in which you took control of a portion of your life. It is likely that didn't turn out so well. On the other hand, you are well aware of situations in which you expected God to intervene, but He didn't.

As you mature in your relationship with God, you'll begin to see things from His perspective. In Isaiah 55:8, God said, "For My thoughts are not your thoughts, and your ways are not My ways." God's view of your life is much different than your view of your life. Some of the struggles and obstacles you face are really God's way of helping you make course corrections.

Think back to a situation that you first thought was bad but later turned out better than you expected. What did you learn about God in that situation?

_____

_____

Based on the closeness of your relationship with God, how certain are you of His plan for your life?

__ totally uncertain

__ I have an idea

__ I know His plan for my life

Read Ephesians 4:11–14. This passage describes the real purpose of our lives. Take a close look at verse 12. No matter what our profession, we all have the same purpose. How is your life fulfilling God's purpose?

_____

_____

God left you on earth for a reason. You have a personal ministry and your church has a responsibility for equipping you for that ministry. Think about your current involvement in your church. How are you being equipped?

_____

_____

Making your life count isn't a one-time experience; it's a way of life. It involves vision and determination. As you think about your vision for your life, what are some ways you see yourself making a difference in the world?

_____

_____

Arrange the ideas above in order of the most reasonable to the most creative. What are some common themes you see running through your list?

_____

_____

Circle the idea that most interests you right now. Keep in mind that making a difference is a way of life; the avenue through which you make a difference might change over time. List some skills or abilities needed to fulfill the circled idea.

_____

_____

What training or information do you need to be fully equipped to achieve this goal?

_____

_____

How can you make a difference in the world through the idea you circled?

_____

_____

How will this idea make God famous?

_____

_____

The Bible tells the stories of ordinary people who were used by God for extraordinary tasks. The "superstars" in the Bible aren't famous because of what they did; they are famous because of what they allowed God to do through their lives.

If you want your life to count, you must keep God at the center of it. He knows how to use you for His glory. By positioning yourself in the center of God's plan, you will discover unconditional love and the abundant life Jesus promised.

INSPIRATIONAL QUOTES FOR
PERSONAL REFLECTION

"I used to be afraid I wouldn't make enough money;
now I'm afraid I won't make enough difference."
—Bob Goff

～

"How wonderful it is that nobody needs wait a single
moment before starting to improve the world."
—Anne Frank

～

"We make a living by what we get, but we make a life
by what we give." —Winston Churchill

～

"It's easy to make a buck. It's a lot tougher to make a
difference." —Tom Brokaw

～

"Being a man or a woman is a matter of birth. Being a man or a woman who makes a difference is a matter of choice." —Byron Garrett

⌒

"The great use of life is to spend it for something that outlasts it." —William James

⌒

"Everybody can be great because anybody can serve. You don't have to have a college degree to serve. You don't have to make your subject and your verb agree to serve. . . . You don't have to know the second theory of thermodynamics in physics to serve. You only need a heart full of grace. A soul generated by love." —Martin Luther King Jr.

⌒

"The world is not interested in what we do for a living. What they are interested in is what we have to offer freely—hope, strength, love, and the power to make a difference!" —Sasha Azevedo

⌒

"I am only one, but still I am one. I cannot do everything, but still I can do something; and because I cannot do everything, I will not refuse to do something that I can do." —Helen Keller

"Never believe that a few caring people can't change the world. For, indeed, that's all who ever have." — Margaret Mead

"When you cease to make a contribution, you begin to die." —Eleanor Roosevelt

"Often we set out to make a difference in the lives of others only to discover we have made a difference in our own." —Ellie Braun-Haley

"The REAL American Dream is not about a garage full of new cars, winning the lottery, or retiring to a life of ease in Florida. It's about doing work that has meaning, work that makes a difference, and doing that work with people you care about." —Joe Tye

"We must not, in trying to think about how we can make a big difference, ignore the small daily differences we can make which, over time, add up to big differences that we often cannot foresee." —Marian Wright Edelman

"Power is the ability to do good things for others."
—Brooke Astor

"At this very moment, there are people only you can reach . . . and differences only you can make."
—Mike Dooley

"Only a life lived for others is a life worthwhile."
—Albert Einstein

"What you do makes a difference, and you have to decide what kind of difference you want to make."
—Jane Goodall

"There is no greater joy nor greater reward than to make a fundamental difference in someone's life."
—Mary Rose McGeady

"You are not here to save the world but you are here to touch the hands that are within your reach."
—Kathleen Price

"Go out and make a difference in your community.
You don't need endless time and perfect conditions.
Do it now. Do it today. Do it for twenty minutes and
watch your heart start beating." —Barbara Sher

"We must overcome the notion that we must be regular
. . . it robs you of the chance to be extraordinary and
leads you to the mediocre." —Uta Hagen

"Whether you live to be fifty or one hundred makes
no difference, if you made no difference in the world."
—Jarod Kintz

"You don't have to know a lot of things for your life to
make a lasting difference in the world.
But you do have to know the few great things that
matter, perhaps just one, and then be willing to live
for them and die for them. The people that make a
durable difference in the world are not the people
who have mastered many things, but who have been
mastered by one great thing." —John Piper

"Everyone thinks of changing the world, but no one thinks of changing himself." —Leo Tolstoy

⌒

"Life shrinks or expands in proportion to one's courage." —Anais Nin

⌒

"The question isn't who is going to let me; it's who is going to stop me." —Ayn Rand

⌒

"Come on, Sam. Remember what Bilbo used to say: 'It's a dangerous business, Frodo, going out your door. You step onto the road, and if you don't keep your feet, there's no knowing where you might be swept off to.'"
—J. R. R. Tolkien

⌒

"In a very real sense not one of us is qualified, but it seems that God continually chooses the most unqualified to do his work, to bear his glory. If we are qualified, we tend to think that we have done the job ourselves. If we are forced to accept our evident lack of qualification, then there's no danger that we will confuse God's work with our own, or God's glory with our own." —Madeleine L'Engle

⌒

"We can't solve problems by using the same kind of thinking we used when we created them."
—Albert Einstein

⌒

"We cannot become what we want to be by remaining what we are." —Max DePree

⌒

"Until you discover your 'fire within' you will remain condemned to a life only endured, not lived; to delicacies only tasted, not devoured; to joys only imagined, not experienced." Alister Cameron

⌒

"All adventures, especially into new territory, are scary." —Sally Ride

⌒

"In these bodies we live and in these bodies we will die. Where you invest your love you invest your life."
—Marcus Mumford

⌒

"True power is an individual's ability to move from failure to failure with no loss of enthusiasm."
—Winston Churchill

⌒

"Practice isn't the thing you do once you're good,
it's the thing you do that makes you good."
—Malcolm Gladwell

"The way to get started is to quit talking
and begin doing." —Walt Disney

"People generally see what they look for and hear what
they listen for." —Harper Lee

"It is not enough to be busy. So are the ants.
The question is: What are we busy about?"
—Henry David Thoreau

"Act as if what you do makes a difference.
Because it does." —William James

SCRIPTURE GUIDE
FOR PERSONAL DEVOTION

Reference	Verse
Psalm 52:8	But I am like a flourishing olive tree in the house of God; I trust in God's faithful love forever and ever.
Psalm 84:1	How lovely is Your dwelling place, LORD of Hosts.
Psalm 98:3	He has remembered His love and faithfulness to the house of Israel; all the ends of the earth have seen our God's victory.
Psalm 107:1	Give thanks to the LORD, for He is good; His faithful love endures forever.
Psalm 136:1	Give thanks to the LORD, for He is good. His love is eternal.
Romans 5:5	This hope does not disappoint, because God's love has been poured out in our hearts through the Holy Spirit who was given to us.

Ephesians 3:17–19	I pray that you, being rooted and firmly established in love, may be able to comprehend with all the saints what is the length and width, height and depth of God's love, and to know the Messiah's love that surpasses knowledge, so you may be filled with all the fullness of God.
Colossians 2:2	I want their hearts to be encouraged and joined together in love, so that they may have all the riches of assured understanding, and have the knowledge of God's mystery—Christ.
Colossians 3:12–13	Therefore, God's chosen ones, holy and loved, put on heartfelt compassion, kindness, humility, gentleness, and patience, accepting one another and forgiving one another if anyone has a complaint against another. Just as the Lord has forgiven you, so also you must forgive.
2 Thessalonians 1:3	We must always thank God for you, brothers, which is fitting, since your faith is flourishing, and the love of every one of you for one another is increasing.

2 Thessalonians 3:5	May the Lord direct your hearts to God's love and Christ's endurance.
1 John 3:1	Look at how great a love the Father has given us, that we should be called God's children. And we are! The reason the world does not know us is that it didn't know Him.
1 John 3:10	This is how God's children—and the Devil's children—are made evident. Whoever does not do what is right is not of God, especially the one who does not love his brother.
1 John 3:17	If anyone has this world's goods and sees his brother in need but shuts off his compassion from him—how can God's love reside in him?
1 John 4:9	God's love was revealed among us in this way: God sent His One and Only Son into the world so that we might live through Him.
1 John 4:20	If anyone says, "I love God," yet hates his brother, he is a liar. For the person who does not love his brother whom he has seen cannot love God whom he has not seen.

1 John 5:2	This is how we know that we love God's children when we love God and obey His commands.
Luke 11:42	But woe to you Pharisees! You give a tenth of mint, rue, and every kind of herb, and you bypass justice and love for God. These things you should have done without neglecting the others.
2 Corinthians 8:7–9	Now as you excel in everything—in faith, in speech, in knowledge, in all diligence, and in your love for us—excel also in this grace. I am not saying this as a command. Rather, by means of the diligence of others, I am testing the genuineness of your love. For you know the grace of our Lord Jesus Christ: although He was rich, for your sake He became poor, so that by His poverty you might become rich.
Psalm 25:10	All the LORD's ways show faithful love and truth to those who keep His covenant and decrees.
Zechariah 7:9	The LORD of Hosts says this: Render true justice. Show faithful love and compassion to one another.

Romans 12:10	Show family affection to one another with brotherly love. Outdo one another in showing honor.
Hebrews 6:10	For God is not unjust; He will not forget your work and the love you showed for His name when you served the saints—and you continue to serve them.
John 13:34–35	I give you a new command: Love one another. Just as I have loved you, you must also love one another. By this all people will know that you are My disciples, if you have love for one another.
Matthew 22:36–40	"Teacher, which commandment in the law is the greatest?" He said to him, "Love the Lord your God with all your heart, with all your soul, and with all your mind. This is the greatest and most important commandment. The second is like it: Love your neighbor as yourself. All the Law and the Prophets depend on these two commandments."
Matthew 5:42	Give to the one who asks you, and don't turn away from the one who wants to borrow from you.

Matthew 5:43–44	You have heard that it was said, Love your neighbor and hate your enemy. But I tell you, love your enemies and pray for those who persecute you.
Mark 12:33	And to love Him with all your heart, with all your understanding, and with all your strength, and to love your neighbor as yourself, is far more important than all the burnt offerings and sacrifices.
Romans 13:9	The commandments: Do not commit adultery, do not murder, do not steal, do not covet, and if there is any other commandment—all are summed up by this: Love your neighbor as yourself.
Galatians 5:14	For the entire law is fulfilled in one statement: Love your neighbor as yourself.
Leviticus 19:18	Do not take revenge or bear a grudge against members of your community, but love your neighbor as yourself; I am the LORD.

Jeremiah 29:11	"For I know the plans I have for you"—this is the LORD's declaration—"plans for your welfare, not for disaster, to give you a future and a hope."
Psalm 33:11	The counsel of the LORD stands forever, the plans of His heart from generation to generation.
Psalm 40:5	LORD my God, You have done many things—Your wonderful works and Your plans for us; none can compare with You. If I were to report and speak of them, they are more than can be told.
Proverbs 15:22	Plans fail when there is no counsel, but with many advisers they succeed.
Proverbs 16:3	Commit your activities to the LORD and your plans will be achieved.
Proverbs 16:9	A man's heart plans his way, but the LORD determines his steps.
Proverbs 19:21	Many plans are in a man's heart, but the LORD's decree will prevail.
Proverbs 21:5	The plans of the diligent certainly lead to profit, but anyone who is reckless only becomes poor.

Isaiah 25:1	LORD, You are my God; I will exalt You. I will praise Your name, for You have accomplished wonders, plans formed long ago, with perfect faithfulness.
Isaiah 29:15	Woe to those who go to great lengths to hide their plans from the LORD. They do their works in darkness, and say, "Who sees us? Who knows us?"
Isaiah 32:8	But a noble person plans noble things; he stands up for noble causes.
Romans 13:14	But put on the Lord Jesus Christ, and make no plans to satisfy the fleshly desires.
Psalm 25:6	Remember, LORD, Your compassion and Your faithful love, for they have existed from antiquity.
Psalm 86:15	But You, Lord, are a compassionate and gracious God, slow to anger and abundant in faithful love and truth.
Psalm 103:4	He redeems your life from the Pit; He crowns you with faithful love and compassion.
Psalm 103:8	The LORD is compassionate and gracious, slow to anger and full of faithful love.

Psalm 116:5	The LORD is gracious and righteous; our God is compassionate.
Matthew 9:36	When He saw the crowds, He felt compassion for them, because they were weary and worn out, like sheep without a shepherd.
1 Peter 3:8–9	Now finally, all of you should be like-minded and sympathetic, should love believers, and be compassionate and humble, not paying back evil for evil or insult for insult but, on the contrary, giving a blessing, since you were called for this, so that you can inherit a blessing.

SUGGESTED READING

Simple Life by Thom and Art Rainer
(ISBN: 9780805448863)

The Power of Persistence by Michael Catt
(ISBN: 9780805448689)

One in a Million by Priscilla Shirer
(ISBN: 9780805464764)

A Hope and a Future by Don Wilton
(ISBN: 9780805445558)

Against All Odds by Chuck Norris
(ISBN: 9780805444216)

Courageous Living by Michael Catt
(ISBN: 9781433671210)

Embracing Obscurity by Anonymous
(ISBN: 9781433677816)

The Five Smooth Stones by Robertson McQuilken
(ISBN: 9780805445183)

God in the Marketplace by Henry and Richard Blackaby
(ISBN: 9780805446883)

God Will by Ken Hemphill
(ISBN: 9780805447682)

Grace Is Enough by Willie Aames and Maylo Upton
(ISBN: 9780805443790)

A Heart Like His by Beth Moore
(ISBN: 9781433677168)

Identity by Eric Geiger
(ISBN: 9780805446890)

Influencing Like Jesus by Michael Zigarelli
(ISBN: 9780805447101)

Jack's Life: The Life Story of C.S. Lewis by Douglas Gresham
(ISBN: 9780805432466)

A Life Well Lived by Tommy Nelson
(ISBN: 9780805440881)

Living Beyond Your Lifetime by Mike Huckabee
(ISBN: 9780805423365)

Living with Less by Mark Tabb
(ISBN: 9780805432961)

Mended by Angie Smith
(ISBN: 9781433676604)

Ten Who Changed the World by Danny L. Akin
(ISBN: 9781433673078)

You Are Gifted by Ken Hemphill
(ISBN: 9780805448627)

Zig Ziglar's Life Lifters by Zig Ziglar
(ISBN: 9780805426892)

The 2 Degree Difference by John Trent
(ISBN: 9780805449839)